THE MIRACLE OF HSIN TAO
THE EASY WAY TO SELF-HEALING AND LONG LIFE

- FOR BEGINNERS -

BY
RATZIEL BANDER

Published by Hsin Tao Institute 2006
© Ratziel Bander 2005. All rights reserved.

ISBN 1-4196-2946-8   Pub Date: Aug-19-2005

For information contact institute@hsintao.com

BOOK DESIGN
OWL ARTS

PHOTOGRAPHS
HUBERTUS SCHÜLER

Dedication

To the keepers of the secrets, to Sri Sathya Sai Baba,
And the exalted lineage of Ho Lo.

Acknowledgements

With heartfelt gratitude to all those who have sponsored, and continue to sponsor this very special work throughout the world.

Many thanks to Ione Linker, Dr. Lauree Moss, Laura Crosta, Simone Niehues and the Hamburgers, Maureen Belaski, and all those who, in their individual ways, made the writing and publishing of this book possible.

Disclaimer

Hsin Tao is not meant to replace medical treatments or procedures. It is not a form of medical diagnosis or therapy, and makes no claims to be such.

People learning and practicing this method are advised to consult an accredited, expert teacher who displays the Hsin Tao trademark, for detailed instruction, analysis and methodology.

People practicing this method directly from the book do so at their own risk.

Those with disabilities or medical conditions are advised to consult their doctor before practicing Hsin Tao. If symptoms persist, consult a medical practitioner.

Contents

PART ONE: THE STORY

PART TWO: THE MOVES

PART THREE: PRACTICE

PART FOUR: TESTIMONIALS

Part One: The Story

*"When Wisdom came to me, all good things came with her.
She brought me untold riches. I was happy with them all, because
Wisdom had brought them to me. I had not realized before that
she was the source of all these things."*

The Wisdom of Solomon 7: 11-12

1. The Gift

It was as if I had been walking in a jeweled garden when, from nowhere, I was handed the most precious gem of all. Not only was this treasure perfect, unique and beyond human value, but it was also mine to keep forever.

Reality had turned to dream, because when I looked closely at this gift, I knew it had a life of its own. Surrounded by a mysterious energy, by wisdom and guardians, it demanded my full attention, protection and nurturing care. Not only that, but if I continued to focus my energies on this priceless jewel, it would begin to heal every part of me and help others in ways I could not then even imagine. This living work of art began to fill every atom of my being, penetrate every cell, and to transform everything it touched. The 'Way of the Gods' was truly God's Grace visiting me here on earth.

2. Divine Intervention

It all began one day, as I sat to meditate in my shrine room. I was exhausted by the physical and emotional ordeals I'd had to muddle through continually for almost eight years. My body was unable to sit in meditation for more than ten minutes at a time without causing damage to itself. Thankfully, I had done so much meditative work in my life that I only needed a few seconds to take my mind into deep meditation.

As I sat absorbed in a type of temporary bliss, a prayer came to my lips,

"Dear God," I whispered. "There must be some exercise I can do to help cure me, or at least help me improve and be in less pain. Something gentle enough not to hurt me, but so effective that it gives me strong results. Please dear One, send me help in this way. Don't abandon me now. After all, haven't I depended on you for so long, for everything? Have you not always been my light and my love? Would it not be a shame to leave me die an ignominious, undignified death, when I have been your lover all my life? Send me some help if you can dear Lord. Do not abandon me now. . ."

Then, two weeks later, the miracle began.

3. The Offer

I had just about finished my consultation with an honorary doctor in a hospital day-treatment clinic. This man was a grand master of Tai Chi and other martial arts, including Chinese sword fighting and Chi Gong. He had been living in my hometown for about 30 years and I had known him casually for about 25 of those years. The hospital had given him an honorary medical doctorate, because he was considered the most authoritative local expert regarding acupuncture and herbal medicine.

We had just finished arguing about whether or not he should prescribe certain herbs for me. I had a serious problem in my lung and refused to take any further tests. Primarily, I was there to get a Chinese Herbal remedy, although he made it clear he did not think herbs, under the circumstances, would do much good. Being extremely headstrong, I had won the argument and he was just finishing writing his prescription.

He knew that I had been fighting post polio syndrome for many years with only marginal success, but I had never really asked for his help with that difficult malady. In fact, he had never shown much interest in post polio syndrome at all, or in any other problem that I was having. He'd always seemed too happy within himself to be concerned with other people's problems.

But this day, as he finished writing his prescription, he turned and said, with his enigmatic Chinese accent,

"I have a technique that has been kept secret for many years. For the past two weeks, I have been thinking that I should come and show it to the people in the mountains. With this technique, you can cure anything. You live in the mountains now don't you?"

I was more than a little surprised, but managed to grunt a suspicious "Yes".

"It is a very simple technique," he continued. "Let me show you. You interested?"

"Ah... yes... yes of course." His offer caught me completely by surprise.

Then, sitting in his chair, he started to go through a series of hand movements that coincided with deliberate breathing, similar to what I knew to be a martial arts type of breath.

He was so relaxed and the movements were so gentle, yet I could feel a warmth emanating from his belly. An energy field seemed to reach out from his centre and touch me, bringing me a sense of peace and stillness similar to what I was used to in deep meditation.

He continued in this way for a few minutes. I was by then thoroughly impressed with the idea that this style of exercise was definitely gentle enough for me to do without damaging myself. If it was even fractionally as effective as he had boasted it to be, then it might just be the answer to my prayer.

"You see?" he glowed, "It's easy." He stressed the word as if it brought him real pleasure.

"It makes me hot, hot. See?" His hand wiped away invisible perspiration from his forehead.

"And then . . . " Standing with his eyes closed, he began to move and sway in a freeform dance, feet rooted to the floor. There appeared to be no sense to what he was doing and certainly, it was not in any way graceful as his previous demonstration had been. It looked instead as if he was clowning about.

"You see?" He seemed tremendously excited about what he was doing.

"When you have mastered the technique, the body begins to move in its own way to heal itself with perfect precision. See?"

I didn't quite see at the time, but he continued in any case.

"This whole thing is very powerful, for regenerating the body, calming the mind and healing yourself. You can do it!" He grinned.

Over the next two years, the Grand Master drove long hours to the mountains, to my home, and taught me a technique that amazed me with its ease and effects. To learn this secret practice, you did not have to be fit or strong, you did not need to stretch, you did need any propensity or ability for exercise at all. It was truly like nothing I had ever learned before.

At the first lesson I was convinced I was being shown just another species of familiar Chinese style exercise, loaded with extremely ambitious promises and tantalizing hopes. Very quickly, however, I learned that this was something unique and special. Within the first two weeks I began to understand how privileged I was to be learning something that had deservedly been cherished and protected as a secret teaching for more than 1,350 years. Now, here in my little mountain home, the secret was being handed to me openly, not only without strings to bind, but it was also being taught with a spirit of release. I was learning not only to heal myself, but also to free the technique of its elite confines. The Grand Master had explained when he first told me about it in the hospital clinic,

"I think it's time it was no longer a secret. It could help many people. You got me?"

4. My Story

At the age of five, one month after receiving a compulsory polio vaccination, I experienced one of the worst seven cases of poliomyelitis recorded in Australia. I was paralyzed from head to toe and had been given up to die. By some miracle, I recovered.

In my teenage years, I exerted enormous determination and effort to rehabilitate myself. I began with yoga at the age of fourteen, then after some time and much pain, I expanded into modern dance techniques. By the age of nineteen, I was healthy and robust. I still dealt with an unusual amount of bodily aches, and depression, but in general, I functioned perfectly.

It was over twenty-five years later that the real trouble with polio began. I had worked my body so hard in order to recover from the initial disease, that by my mid-thirties, a whole new set of degenerative symptoms sprang to life. Because they came unheralded, they were much more worrying than the actual polio. It was only after approximately four years of painful degeneration, that doctors were able to diagnose 'Post Polio Syndrome'.

Post Polio Syndrome (PPS) is a condition that stems from

the nervous system. It can affect almost all bodily systems: digestion and absorption; immune system; muscle, bone and spine; emotions. Too much exercise can cause further degeneration, too little can have the same result. Damage to the body can be dramatic and long-lasting and can be caused by even the slightest bump. A PPS sufferer experiences pain sometimes at three times the intensity of a normal body. They heal up to nine times slower than others, whilst often being unreasonably jumpy, irritable, depressed and angry.

By the age of forty-three my symptoms were severe. Although my spiritual practices since the age of fourteen kept me moderately calm, nothing I did was able to stem the physical deterioration. A stream of professionals had only exacerbated the condition. Any sort of orthodox medication – even aspirin - had disastrous side effects. I was left with only what doctors called 'pain management' to make life more bearable. Thankfully, my spiritual background made this quite possible. Whereas others might give in altogether to their anger and frustration, I somehow maintained a degree of detachment, especially in the worst moments of crisis.

During my career, I had trained dancers, actors, and singers in corrective exercise and breathing. I had taught yoga, meditation and movement. My adult education included Tai Chi, Chi Gong, and Tantra, as well as other less well-known disciplines. In those last few years, none of my knowledge could reverse the syndrome. Even the most gentle yoga asana[1] was too demanding, invariably causing further damage.

HSIN TAO

My muscles twitched incessantly. There was always pain in some section of the body. I was so weak that I found it difficult to brush my teeth. Holding a book up whilst lying in bed was a real project, and often a painful one. I could not sit for more than ten minutes at a time, nor could I stand for any longer. Walking for twenty minutes meant I was having a good day.

I had long lost the ability to lie on my back without experiencing excruciating pain. Colds and flu's were my constant companions. There were prostate, urinary tract, and bladder problems. If I ejaculated, I was hit by a doubled onslaught of symptoms.

Most inconvenient were the massive spasms that wracked through my torso without any warning. These occurred with irregular frequency, leaving me on the floor in an indescribable agony, unable to walk for up to four weeks at a time. Worst were the times I had not fully recovered from one, when the next struck, prolonging the whole debacle. Finally, to add a touch of impending doom to the picture, I discovered a serious problem in the lung.

In short, I was a pathetic wreck, and my wife was a stoic. She took over all aspects of practical life, including lifting, carrying, and household chores. As she told me many times, it was easier for her to do these things than see me go into another of those spasms that left me bedridden and of even less help around the house. I found myself tormented by an ill-fated life of luxury.

5. The Miracle Begins

After the first day of practicing Hsin Tao, I felt a different sort of energy in my body. It wasn't so much that I was full of vigor, but I did not feel completely drained either, a state to which I had become accustomed. Things got steadily better from that point. Within a week I was noticeably in much less pain. This progress, minor though it may have been, made me very keen to continue. Until that time nothing had achieved such results. After two weeks, I could brush my teeth with ease. Within three weeks, I could hold a book without stressing my arms. Six weeks, and I realized that, without even noticing, I had been painlessly lying on my back, for the first time in eighteen months! These seemingly petty improvements were like miracles to me and meant a major change in my life. While it had taken eight years to arrive at such a state of decrepitude, it had only taken three weeks to reverse the tide.

I continued to practice, twice a day, in earnest.

Even when I was in great pain, or was incapacitated by a spasm, I still could manage to perform the exercises without hurting myself. I had to make the movements very small, but even so, they continued to cause improvement.

The first time I struggled to my feet whilst convalescing from a spasm in order to practice the first standing exercise, was the most memorable. I found that, although I could barely walk, I could still make the simple movement coupled with its breath. It was a fascinating thing to experience. And although I was in awful pain whenever I tried to walk or sit, whilst I did the exercise the pain vanished. I could only keep it up for about five minutes, but that was obviously enough.

After two weeks of doing that short routine twice a day I was out of the crisis. Before this, my recovery from a spasm was usually three to four weeks! I could hardly believe it. In the past, I had tried exercise, massage and bodywork, physiotherapy, herbs and homeopathy, none of which had improved the recovery rate. Indeed, such tactics had often slowed the recovery rate down, or had caused another spasm.

What most fascinated me was the mystery as to why these exercises worked at all. Their most astonishing feature is the lack of effort. Other techniques such as Feldenkreis and Alexander technique also work on a minimal, effortless premise, but the Hsin Tao movements are not anywhere near as precise, detailed, or logical. One does not have to be an expert, or work closely with an expert to get real results. My improvements came after one lesson. I practiced every day after that, but did not see my teacher again for another six months. By the end of those six months, I was a changed person.

I had learnt and practiced many physical and mental techniques in my life, but I had never experienced such progressive outcomes from such little work. My wife and I, both experiencing quite different and individual results, were mystified. Often we would try to work out why these strange and beautiful movements had such profound effects. They seemed so insubstantial. Sometimes we could make sense of it according to Chinese medical theory, but often we would be at a loss, and left in awe.

My body was improving beyond all possibilities. Even my lung felt easier. Almost daily I became noticeably calmer. My mind started to clear, I was thinking more reasonably and was lifted out of a depression that had haunted me most of my life. With the onslaught of PPS I had experienced periods of serious misery, anger and a feeling of hopelessness. Many times, I felt emotionally exhausted, just by the thought of having to put up with another day of pain and incapacity.

As I became lighter, at peace, I would occasionally drift into a state of ecstasy whilst doing the exercises. It was becoming easier to accept what had happened to me and who I was. I did not feel perpetually agitated and angry, and there were many less panic attacks. Over time, I was transforming into who I wanted to be, rather than feeling that I was one person on the outside – the one who dealt with people and day to day business – and another internal, idealistic person, that only God and my closest friends knew. More and more, I was able to live out the hidden side of myself without fear or embarrassment, falling ever more obviously in love with God and His divine mysteries. Spontaneously, I became more easily immersed in my inner being, without recourse to any philosophy or religion. It just happened. I suppose you could say I gradually 'came out of the closet'. The 'me' I had been hiding for fear of persecution, was gaining strength, while old patterns were fading away.

Although I was pleased with this improvement, there was still a certain reservation. After all, how far can one really improve from a physical condition for which there is medically no cure, and a degenerative prognosis? I made myself content just to experience more mobility and less pain. I never thought it could go much further.

During our second visit from the Grand Master, he had said to me,

"You practice this twice a day for nine months and you'll see that everything will change."

As I had never been a fan of the 'New Age' style sell-you-a-positive-future-in-one-easy-lesson approach, when I heard this promise I was skeptical to say the least.

A year after our first lesson, as my wife and I sat at the dining table reviewing the tremendous progress that I had made, we remembered this prediction that the Grand Master had made. Thinking back, we realized that not only had both our health states improved dramatically, but so had our lives in total. It wasn't just within ourselves, feeling emotionally more at peace, physically stronger, more resilient and active, but our environment had changed in a way that was much more harmonious and enriching. We couldn't explain how the change came about, but life had definitely evolved more happily. We still lived in the same house, but otherwise everything, as he said, had changed. How could a simple exercise do all that? Perhaps it was just a coincidence. Nevertheless, it presented a fascinating mystery.

Two years after we began to practice, I had witnessed an eighty percent recovery. Occasionally the spasms still rocked me, but they were much less frequent, less intense, and the after effects only lasted days, instead of weeks.

I still found the lack of effort I had to put into the exercises incredible. In fact they made me very hot, and almost every session I worked up a sweat without any real exertion, which calmed and refreshed me, in a way similar to the feeling I used to get after an intense hour of Hatha Yoga. The difference being that I need only spend ten to twenty effortless minutes practicing Hsin Tao to achieve that same type of feeling, which lasted the whole day. As I write this book, almost seven years later, I am still aware that the improvements to my health appear endless. At age fifty, I should be noticing some sort of decline. Instead, I feel stronger, calmer, more resilient, virile and active than I have been for the past fifteen years. The fascination and mystery continues. The sense of inner peace grows.

It was at that two-year interval that the Grand Master came to my home in the mountains for the last time. He taught me many things that day. As he left, with a delighted smile and a slightly surprised ring in his voice, he congratulated me. He had observed that I was just about ready to go out and teach Hsin Tao.

I had been a teacher many times, but I was a little perplexed as to how I would go about teaching a totally unknown method to a world that, basically, knew nothing about it or me. After all, I had been retired for about eight years, and had lost my once all-important 'connections'. Certainly, there appeared to be very little interest in my hometown.

Nevertheless, I set about reformulating the technique for western sensibilities. I knew from my years of working with herbs that the method of administering Chinese herbs to Westerners was different from that used with Chinese people. The Westerners had to be given different dosages, over a different time scale to the Chinese. I was not sure why this was so important, other than the herbs had a greater effect this way. They were more easily assimilated. For some reason the Western body could not integrate Chinese herbs in the same way as the Chinese.

I reasoned that these exercises were in fact a type of medicine that should also be administered with specific dosages for Westerners. It was understood that the Grand Master had given me this work to disseminate, because I had assimilated the techniques quickly and effortlessly. Now I was faced with the challenge of making the Hsin Tao accessible to the Western mind and body. The Grand Master could not help me with this. He was too busy with other projects and showed no inclination. It was clear that it would be up to me to take this further. He had given me the technique; I had understood and received the transmission; his job was done..."I gave you these techniques, now its up to you."

The teaching method I had developed over a period of twenty-five years helped soften the learning impact of the Hsin Tao method. Although I maintained the movements with absolute authenticity, the approach became supportive, encouraging, and deep with explanations, both on the physical and psychological substance of the work. This was a departure from the way that I was taught – a type of get-it-now-or-don't-get-it-at-all approach, delivered with a certain terseness, and lack of involvement, designed to weed out devoted students from those with less capacity to endure the rigors of self-imposed discipline.

One day, when I was describing my understanding of the exercises, imbued with the westernized approach to the Grand Master, he asked me with a twinkle in his eye, "How do you know so much?" I replied that he must be an excellent teacher.

I felt ready, yet I was perplexed as to how I could share this new, and increasingly deep knowledge with other people.

When a famous psychic channel told me I had a big job coming up, that I was going to teach in all parts of the world, starting with America, all I could do was laugh. I envisaged myself, a parochial Australian, getting off the plane in the formidable USA, where I knew not one soul, and announcing to no one in particular that I was there to teach Hsin Tao! The mere idea was ridiculous. It was the stuff of pipe dreams, and too daunting a prospect to even consider. I just kept quietly practicing, relying more and more on the invisible, healing energies that were welling up inside of me, allowing myself to be myself.

A few months later, like a whirlwind, the journey began.

6. Beginning the Mission

First, I was invited to Bali. It was there, in the remote hills, that an Oracle of Sai Baba told me the whole story of what was to follow. "You will travel the world, teaching from your experience, bringing people peace." It is interesting, in light of her prediction, that the most common feedback I receive after teaching Hsin Tao is the practicing students' ongoing feeling of inner peace. This seems to apply to most of the students whether they are high-powered executives, or meditation practitioners. The first result that people experience, is a feeling of inner quiet that leads to peace.

My travels taught me more about Hsin Tao than I could have imagined. In Bali I worked with a weight lifter who, after a week of practicing the first gentle standing move of Hsin Tao, made me sit and watch a session of weight lifting in the improvised semi outdoor gym he and his friends had piled together. He explained that if he practiced Hsin Tao for ten minutes immediately before the weight lifting session, his ability to work the bench press increased by a third. He demonstrated, pressing up a massive block of weights thirty times. Sweating and trembling under the strain of the last lift, he assured me that before he had learnt Hsin

Tao, he could only do twenty of the same presses. What caught his attention was the almost instantaneous improvement. One day twenty, the next thirty. The usual gradual development had not applied. The day he practiced Hsin Tao before his usual work out, an extra ten presses came as a complete surprise. He was unsure whether he'd made a mistake, but next day the results were the same.

Bali was wonderful, but I didn't teach there very much. I spent most of my time drifting, enjoying my improving health, the tropical heat and careless way of life.

It was September 11, 2001. I watched the NYC Twin Towers attack on cable television at a friend's bungalow. Within a week, I received a call from Australia, offering me tickets to Los Vegas with spending money. Two weeks later, I was in the USA.

In Los Angeles, I was introduced to the 'mother of rebirthing', Sondra Ray. She insisted I present my work at one of her seminars. After the first demonstration, there was an overwhelming demand for me to pass the teachings on. And so, I began to learn more about Hsin Tao.

In the course of my time there, I worked with a diversity of people and symptoms.

The exercises helped people with back problems. One person came to me with a slipped disk and a split disk, with which she had been living for ten years. She did not want to undergo surgery, so she had been practicing pain management, much as I had when in the deepest throws of PPS. I saw her at least once, sometimes twice a week for six weeks, and the transformation was staggering. From a woman who had very little mobility, she very quickly acquired a range of easy movement. She could walk longer distances, and most profound, in her mind, she felt calmer than she could ever remember. This progress was not without pain, but as she explained, this was the first thing she was able to do that did not exacerbate her condition. She had tried many exercise therapies, but had given up, relying instead on Chiropractic, Rolfing, and Massage on a weekly basis to keep her mobile. The Hsin Tao had made her self reliant, calm, and more easily active. This woman was a respected and vastly experienced psychotherapist. Through her, I was introduced to other psychotherapists.

One of these people asked me to see a client of hers, who suffered from a type of clinical depression. The hour I spent with her promised to be very delicate, because the smallest 'trigger' could send this once highly successful businesswoman into a dangerous downward spiral. I chose one of the exercises reputed to 'heal the heart'. During the first session she suddenly broke through. She told me that although she could feel that terrible emotional pain rising up inside her, for the first time she felt it was not able to overwhelm her. What was more remarkable, her improvement never abated from that moment forth. Not only did she regain her previous self-composure within weeks, she improved to a state that she described as more confident and grounded than she had ever been before. All this was achieved with no drugs and no complicated procedures. She simply worked with the one exercise until she felt the need to expand her practice. Her psychologist, the 'Chair' of an international association of somatic psychotherapists, was convinced of the power of Hsin Tao to the extent that she herself booked sessions with me every week.

The varied and surprising results continued. I worked with one man in his thirties who had been puffing on asthma drugs for twenty years. His asthma was so severe, that he usually needed four puffs, four times a day to get by: in times of stress, or bad pollution days, he needed more. Within two weeks of working with him, he was down to half a puff, every four days. It amazed him as much as it intrigued me. In the months to come, he stopped practicing Hsin Tao, and his asthma did return. Incredibly, it never regained its previous virulence. Even after four months of no practice, the puffer was used only once every second day. After twenty years of asthma drugs four times a day this was, to him, a minor miracle. Nevertheless, I lamented that he had let his practice go when it had brought such dramatic change, and reminded him that my own improvement had never stopped. Why should he limit his potential to improve, by doing only so much? Apparently, my argument was convincing. He began his practice again, and within two months lost the need for his puffer altogether.

One woman came to me with knee problems. I gave her one session demonstrating how not to strain, and left her to practice. After two months, she contacted me to say that her knees had fully recovered.

Many men have reported that their sex drive and performance increased after the first day of exercise. One man reported that he had to stop doing the exercises because his libido had increased to a level that made him feel uncomfortable. Older men I spoke to had re-experienced the healthy, normal function of waking up each morning with a strong erection: a phenomenon that many had ceased to experience since their late thirties. One man reported gleefully that his libido had jumped dramatically only ten minutes after he had first practiced!

Not only men reported increased sexual desire and ability. Women too are affected in this way, experiencing greater libido, lubrication, and relaxation. A number of post-menopausal women have reported a return of natural vaginal lubrication, some permanently, others periodically.

Others have reported giving up smoking and other addictions with ease. In fact, some simply forget to indulge. One gentleman in his forties neglected to drink his habitual coffee for almost a week before he realized he had unwittingly given it up.

Someone asked for my help after a ten-year court battle had driven her to a state of paranoia. She imagined (rightly, or wrongly) whole armies of people conspiring to ruin her life. Thinking 'they' were tapping her phone calls, surrounding her home with poisons and other extremely high-tech assaults, and using every means available to destroy her health and mental well being. She had become high-strung, nervous, physically depleted and obsessed, unable to relax for even a moment. After three weeks, not only had her health improved to an astonishing degree, but she had also become calm and confident again. Her life changed so radically, that she was able to laugh at what before she had considered life threatening, whilst the court case became almost insignificant to her. Once again, the improvement continued for months to come.

The list of applications for Hsin Tao just kept growing. It increased even further, when I was invited to Britain and Europe to help people with very different cultural backgrounds.

A seventy-year-old gentleman came to one of my workshops. He was very feeble, barely able to stand for fifteen minutes at a time. He suffered from a herniated disc, and a spur in his neck. He could only practice the standing technique for five minutes before having to sit and rest. For years, he had shunned doctor's advice to have an operation. Yet, two weeks after the workshop he reported being able to give up his pain control medication. He started to feel stronger and more agile. Without trying, he found himself standing straighter, and has reported being on a general upward spiral ever since. He practices daily, and last I heard was spending twenty to thirty minutes on each session.

I have received reports of improvement in bladder control; migraine; lower back pain; arthritis; stiff joints; overly flexible vertebrae; nerve damage; general weakness; fatigue; sleeplessness; physical balance; tinnitus; memory; emotional disturbance; panic attacks and stress - as well as some truly exceptional recoveries. All this feedback giving me further confirmation of the power inherent in these simple, once secret movements.

One man in his late thirties came to me with excruciating pain in his left arm. The doctors' diagnosis was that the main nerve fibers going down his arm were being pressed and squeezed because of an overly small aperture in the bone, in the area of the shoulder. They reasoned that the condition was genetic, and the only remedy was to scrape the aperture to enlarge it, thus freeing the nerve fiber. The dangers of this procedure lay in further aggravating the nerve fibers, leading to potentially serious consequences. This man had refused to consider the surgical solution. The risks were too high. For two years he had traveled from practitioner to practitioner, trying almost every known method of body therapy, from the orthodox to the 'way out'. He practiced 'supportive yoga' every day to bring some relief, but in general, he was sent into writhing agony many times throughout the day. Nerve pain is one of the most terrible experiences.

I really didn't know what to do specifically about this man's arm. It was apparent to me in the first moments that this was truly nerve pain, although he was offering all sorts of possibilities. I knew from experience that Hsin Tao worked very powerfully on the central nervous system – in fact, many of the recoveries I had witnessed had, in my opinion, stemmed from conditioning the nervous system first. I started him on the first basic exercise, showing him in great detail how to be very careful. We reduced his effort week by week, until his exertion level was much less than he would use in a very gentle yoga class. In the first three days, we had a definite improvement. Then we hit the 'roller-coaster' syndrome, which in my observation, is part of the natural healing process. Predictably, when his condition declined, it became very much worse than it had been when he first came to see me. Having virtually exhausted all his other options, he chose to continue to work with Hsin Tao. He improved and declined a number of times in the following weeks. His improvements were of such a nature, that he became enthusiastic about the possible outcome. Unfortunately, every time he felt better he would go back and play a game of tennis, or go to a yoga class, or some other sport activity that he truly loved as a pastime. Invariably, each time he ventured back into the world of athletic exertion, no matter how gentle he thought he was being, he would throw himself back into an unrelenting pain. Since he was getting used to being without pain, every time he regressed his spirits sagged more dramatically, which compounded his problem. We continued. At a certain point he began to trust me enough to follow my advice and stop all his other activities, at least until he had experienced no pain for a whole month. In any case, I convinced him that his favorite, tennis, with its jarring movements, would have to go altogether.

He would do well for two or three weeks at a time, but never made it through the full month without pain. Unfortunately, he would decide to speed up the process by going for a treatment, or a massage, which led to disastrous results. The last time this happened, he was in such desperate agony, that he could barely talk. Thankfully, I convinced him to temporarily stop allowing people to give him treatments. I had experienced this sort of dynamic myself when I was being lifted out of the PPS trough.

Each time he went into a decline, I showed him how to make less effort in his Hsin Tao practice, until one day he said,

"I get it! You work way below what you're capable of. Its

almost as if you don't have to move at all, but you're always moving!" From this time on, he was able to maintain his improvement. He began to feel more secure, no longer fearing that the wrong move would plunge him back into pain. At this time, I advised him to go to a cranial/sacral practitioner and insist that all they do is relieve the pressure from his skull. Under no circumstances were they to do anything to his sacrum. The exercises and the natural healing power of his body were taking care of that. He had learnt by now to follow my advice.

It was a full month and he had not returned to pain. Not only that, he told me that the process he had been through with Hsin Tao changed his whole way of doing business. Being an extremely high level, high-powered sales person, with a huge staff and international travel on a weekly basis, he had always pushed himself to the extremes of his ability. Now, he told me, he had learnt a new approach, and understood how to work below his limits. The fact that he could exert himself to a certain degree did not mean he had to. He discovered, just as I had, that major positive changes occurred when he made least effort. Not only did he feel physically better for it, but by applying this lesson to his daily life, his business had also improved. He had found the fine line between flowing with your own innate ability, and pushing yourself beyond the level of real effectiveness. Being still in the midst of chaos, letting the natural flow guide you, is good business, as well as good spiritual practice. Even in the modern, high-end business world, "less is more".

What was interesting to observe, was that he did not learn

this lesson with his mind and apply it intellectually to his life and exercises. Through the Hsin Tao movements, his body had learnt organically what philosophers down the centuries have tried to explain to errant minds. The body had naturally, through a sort of osmosis of consciousness, informed his conscious mind. Only then did he realize that his behavior had changed. It took some months for the lesson to be absorbed by the body and be spontaneously passed on to his 'way of thinking'. Yet, if approached from an intellectual perspective, the same lesson might have taken years of meditative, spiritual, and even philosophical practice, before it could be effectively applied to his daily life.

Another case that I find fascinating is that of a woman who came to me in a wheelchair suffering from spina bifida. Although many of the Hsin Tao exercises are performed whilst sitting, I felt this woman needed more. So I interpreted the first standing movement as a seated exercise for her. This was a highly educated and well-informed woman, with a serious scientific background. She had pursued many avenues of therapy and self-healing, displaying a great deal more specific knowledge than I possessed. Obviously, her major problem was being unable to use her legs, but there were a number of other symptoms that, if addressed would make her life possibly more tolerable.

Although extremely strong in the upper body, if she leaned forward in her wheel chair, she would lose control, and in a spinning motion, fall to the floor. There seemed to be a complete lack of connection between the torso and the pelvic floor, even though she had worked on this area with professionals for many years.

When I showed her what to do with her pelvis, it was a huge challenge for her. There were scant moments when she could just make the connection and feel the smooth movement of the pelvic floor, but she could not maintain it for more than a moment or two. Within a few days of gentle practice, she was able to sustain the connections.

Four months later, she was able to take the exercise to its next level. She demonstrated with ease how she could now lean all the way forward in her wheelchair, maintaining effortless control. There was no longer any risk of falling. She explained, in very clear technical terms, the way she now felt more connected to her legs, whereas before, they were no more than dead lumps. Her thighs felt stronger, and the feet, which had for years been completely numb and icy cold, were now warm. Sometimes, she could even feel tingling on the soles. To me, this was a minor miracle, one of the most moving experiences in my journey as a teacher.

Not only were the physical effects dramatic, she had changed her behavior and temperament in a way that made friends very happy. Being an active and strong woman, her confinement to a wheelchair was irritating and frustrating. She was known for her razor wit and short temper. Her idea of defense was uninhibited attack.

In four months, she became noticeably softer, more tolerant, and less prone to use her formidable intellect to destroy people. This new 'softness' astonished her friends. She explained it as a growing sense of inner peace.

Two people, both suffering with Fibromyalgia and Lupus came to see me. Although they did not know each other and one case was far more advanced than the other, they both experienced similar types of improvement within themselves after working with me for a number of months. The exercises brought physical and emotional benefits, but what was most dramatic for both was a sense of being able to take charge of their lives once again, after many years of feeling victim to their diseases. This sense of being able to regain control of one's life was a very powerful experience for me as well, when I first learned the techniques. Judging from the feedback I have received, this re-establishment of control is a common experience among practitioners coming from a physically or emotionally challenged background. This, in itself, leads to greater self-esteem and confidence in dealing, not only with one's personal problems, but also with the world at large.

An active and fit woman in her late fifties decided she was going on a fifty-mile bicycle ride. In preparation, part of her two-month training regimen was Hsin Tao a number of times a week. She told me that including Hsin Tao was the only part of her workout that was different from her normal get fit program, and she was amazed at how fast she was able to improve stamina, strength and endurance. She had never experienced such rapid and effortless improvement in her sports performance.

After some years of my teaching the method, a number of Martial Arts practitioners have started to come and test the technique. They weighed it against what they already knew and understood of the many different martial arts. Although invariably they started by identifying Hsin Tao as another form of Chi Gong, or other 'soft' martial style that may be familiar, if they practiced for even a short time, without exception they told me that this is something unique. Often they found that it took them to a deeper understanding of the martial art they already knew.

Even 'Power Yoga'[2] practitioners, those devotees of extreme physical exertion, have come to discover the benefits of Hsin Tao. I remember one woman who had been practicing Power Yoga for five years. I advised her to give the Power Yoga a break for a couple of weeks, just to see what Hsin Tao could do for her. Reluctantly, she practiced only the movements I gave her for a fortnight. She told me that when she went back to her Power Yoga it was easier than she had ever experienced. For the first time it was not a strain. Instead, she could approach the tremendously strenuous hour with ease and lightness, achieving much more, with much less effort.

So the list continues. Certainly, these simple exercises cause you to feel hot and even to work up a sweat, without strain or effort. Perhaps the hardest element to learn within these techniques is how not to make an effort. That said, many people feel they have done a complete workout after a relaxed session of Hsin Tao. The feedback continues to amaze me.

Although Hsin Tao works differently on everybody, the most universal effect is the feeling of calm, coupled with a lightness and alertness of mind. If this were the only result of Hsin Tao, it would be an extremely valuable tool.

As it stands, from the feedback of others and from my own experience, it is a precious and unique gift of healing. So precious, that I can easily understand why the monks of Shaolin reputedly kept it secret and revered for over a millennium.

7. The Myth

The origin of Hsin Tao is the stuff of legend. Yet, we must remember that all legends hold more than just conventional truth.

I listened with fascination to the story of Ta Mo, a Buddhist monk, who is said to have lived about 1350 years ago. This monk is well known in some modern circles. Students of Kung Fu know him as Bodhi Dharma, and he is known not only as the originator of Kung Fu and other Wu Shu (fighting styles) of Shaolin, but he is also recognized as the man who introduced 'Zen' ('Chan') to China.

Ta Mo was the only Buddhist monk of his time to travel to Mainland China by sea. In those primitive sailing vessels, endurance, confidence and faith were necessary additions to the seafarer's kit. He visited many island kingdoms on his journey, including the Indonesian Archipelago, traveling through exotic kingdoms, wealthy and colorful, steeped in ancient animist rites, and dominated by the Hindu doctrines, which manifested miracles and peerless saints.

After months negotiating the seas and the different kingdoms along the way, land journey was fraught with danger, uncertainty, and incomprehensible languages. Although he knew his destination, Ta Mo plunged head long into the unknown. It was indeed an undertaking of magnificent daring and endurance. Yet it was more than faith and endurance that drew this man to his destination.

When he finally arrived in China, his saintliness and lightness of mind enabled him to float up the Yangzte River on a leaf. The wind, blowing against the tide, guided him mysteriously to unforeseen destinations.

He preached the Buddhist Dharma wherever he went, with little success. In his zeal, he even offended the Emperor with an uninhibited and original bent on Buddhist teachings.

At last, his travels brought him to a monastery hidden in the mountains at Shaolin. This was an area where Confucianism, Taoism, and finally Buddhism, had only recently taken hold. The area was steeped in ancient, indigenous religious ideas - mysterious practices that included Alchemy, Animism, and a strong cult of Immortality. Taoism, Confucianism, and the pagan cults, were an overt influence in the remote Shaolin Monastery, although it was officially dedicated to the Buddha.

Ta Mo could not gain access here. His status as a Buddhist monk from India, albeit the son of a wealthy Prince, meant nothing to the elite monks of Shaolin. Try as he may, the doorkeeper simply would not let him enter.

Disenchanted with his lack of success, and reasoning that it was due to his own lack of deep understanding, he decided to sit in meditation until he achieved true insight and perhaps even Buddha-hood. A cave nearby would suit him perfectly.

He sat in his cave, unmoving, for nine years. Many believe that the spiritual gaze of his blue eyes bored a hole in the cave wall. Such was the force of Ta Mo's austerity.

When at last he stood up, he was indeed a Buddha - the Buddha Bodhi. From his enlightened state, he gazed down at his body, ravaged and stiff from interminable stillness. He was little more than a living corpse. Yet having gained true insight, he understood that an enlightened being with a sickly body and an absent mind, was not really much use to the world.

So, following the great flow of cosmic energy with which he had merged, he began to move in circles, creating a kind of sacred dance to regenerate both his body and mind, and bring his spirit into full presence within the physical form. These movements, performed whilst standing and sitting, miraculously rejuvenated him.

The once cynical Shaolin monks were by now thoroughly impressed.

Buddha Bodhi was finally welcomed into the monastery as a great soul. Not only did he inspire the residents with his lucid insights and instruction, but he also taught the ailing monks his series of self-healing movements.

The monks of Shaolin had led a sedentary life, spending long hours translating Buddhist texts, and meditating. They were unhealthy, too weak to fulfill the rigorous meditations required by traditional Buddhist sects. Ta Mo explained that one had to be fit and healthy to perform the rites Buddha Sakyamuni had lain down. Indeed, the Buddha Himself had discovered the pitfalls of a weakened body.

The Buddha Bodhi's series of movements, which he categorized into three sections, brought the monks speedily into a state of good health. His exercises and philosophy influenced the entire regimen of the monastery. In particular, the exercises, which enhanced rather than distracted from meditation whilst bringing the body into a state of robust health, became the foundation for all their future success. From that time forth, they preserved these as the secret treasure of Shaolin, and handed them down to only the most senior monks.

Adherence to the system of exercises took some of these monks to a state beyond the restraints of mortality. The masters of Buddha Bodhi's secret system were said to become 'like gods'. They satisfied all the criteria for the ancient and popular cult of immortality. Hence, the system, known exclusively within the monastery walls by a select few, has been handed down to us as the Tao (the Way) of the gods. Not gods that lived in heaven, rather they were immortals who resided on earth. The title refers specifically to the men who practiced for many hours a day in the mountains,[3] perfecting themselves

Tao also has another meaning. Although it is commonly translated as the 'Way' or the 'right path to follow', its deeper esoteric meaning is far more profound. It evokes an indefinable, transcendent perfection. In the West we loosely refer to this presence as God, but it may be more rightly called The Absolute, which resides within us, and without. In this sense, Tao is impossible to accurately describe. It can only be understood by direct experience. It is the path, yet it is also goal of the path - the experience of Absolute Being.

Having achieved this state of perfection, these 'immortals' would 'die into the realm of the gods'. That means that when they died, their consciousness, or their spirit, would ascend into the heavenly realm reserved for the gods, the Brahmaloka, where they could live for eternity – truly immortal.

Sometimes however, they returned to earth, being born once again as humans, but with the secret knowledge of Hsin Tao embedded deep within their consciousness. Here on earth they would find their way once more to a teacher of the Way of the Immortals. They would first re-learn, then teach the ancient Hsin Tao to other highly evolved souls. So the lineage continued for centuries. Not as other lineages go, from master to disciple, but from master to reborn master. True understanding of Hsin Tao has always involved descent from Brahmaloka, the heavenly realm into which all striving souls seek to be reborn.

Within the confines of the Shaolin Monastery, only the senior monks could receive the entire teaching. Such a state of revered excellence was achieved in this practice, that it became known as 'The Art of the Enlightened One'.

During a period of several hundred years after Buddha Bodhi left the Monastery, the Shaolin Monks developed these sacred healing movements into self-defense and Martial Arts. Although fighting styles already existed in China, the monks of Shaolin developed their own highly distinctive defensive arts from Ta Mo's seed movements – his Way of the gods. Shaolin Monks have been known ever since for their almost supernatural powers.

From the time of the Boxer Rebellion, at the beginning of the 20th century, through the Communist revolution, many of the masters were forced to flee the Shaolin Monasteries. Political pressure and persecution made a Shaolin monk's life dangerous and uncertain. The Liberation Army and the opposing Nationalists both routinely slaughtered Monks. Many fled to hide in the mountains, or cross the border, leaving China altogether. Some took with them the precious secrets of Hsin Tao. Finally, during the 'Cultural Revolution', Shaolin was outlawed. The monasteries, including the original in Henan, were either closed or destroyed.

Throughout the years of exile, Hsin Tao continued to remain the stuff of legends, acquiring various mysterious names and enigmatic references. Although only very few were ever taught the authentic technique, the method of transmission continued. Practitioners became a loosely associated elite, roaming freely outside of the communist regime. Hsin Tao practitioners were no longer exclusively members of the Shaolin aristocracy. Yet, they had to have some very special attributes to be handed the teachings.

The secrecy of Hsin Tao was maintained, although no longer to protect the power of the Shaolin monastic system. It continued to be practiced in privacy as a mark of respect for something very precious, for which the world at large was not yet ready to receive. Those chosen to learn had remarkable inherent abilities. They guarded the teachings in purity and authenticity, while the world changed around them: social structures and taboos came tumbling down as an elevated awareness seeped slowly into human consciousness.

Guarding the secrets was finally no longer as important as spreading light, love, and healing to a world straining to grow beyond the bounds of personal power, self glory, and self gratification.

One 'Grand Master', a 'god' to his to students, who resided quietly in British Honk Kong, realized that a new era was arising, that would engender many unknown changes. So, he waited to see just what would happen, and what new destiny awaited the precious Hsin Tao.

In the early 1970's his very special pupil, a true incarnation of compassion, still a young man in his thirties, was sent to Australia – to live and thrive, among the 'barbarians' of the south. Almost thirty years later, that 'young man' became my very special teacher[4].

Part Two: The Moves

Building the Internal Fire

Breathing to regenerate and increase Spirit

Building the Internal Fire is the beginning of the exercise to rejuvenate and increase spirit in the body. This is basically a breathing technique. Note that throughout the exercise, the breath is silent.

This technique rebuilds the body's essence. It increases the store of essential fluid, whilst making the body more resilient to disease. It warms the lower energy centre of the body giving more fundamental strength to the body's core.

Preparation:

• Sit on a cushion of the floor with the legs crossed, or on a chair with the feet flat on the floor.

• Rest the hands on the knees.

• Imagine a point in the centre of the forehead. We call this point the heavenly eye. One inch above the third eye, this point is used to draw energy from "heaven" into the body.

• Expand the belly and allow the body to gently rock backward whilst you allow the breath in through the nose.

• While rocking backwards, imagine energy from "heaven" pouring in from the heavenly eye, filling the lower abdomen.

• Wait for a moment. Allow the breath to sit in the body comfortably. Keep the lower abdomen expanded.

• Allow the belly to collapse and sway forward. Let the breath slowly float out through the nostrils.

• Repeat: expand the belly, rock backwards. Drawing energy from heaven while you breath in, filling the lower abdomen.

• Continue with the in and out breath, drawing energy in through the fourth eye and feeding it down to the belly.

Note: Try breathing in to a count of three, wait for a count of four. Breathe out to a count of six.

The Saint Stretches His Waist

The standing techniques for beginners – to regenerate/rejuvenate the body.

Saint Stretches His Waist is the first of the exercises intended to regenerate the body.

The Saint Stretches His Waist is divided into three sections. Make sure you do all three sections whenever practicing. This exercise tones the spine, massages all of the eternal organs, and brings heat, moisture and energy flow back to the body.

Be careful not to strain the thighs or use the arms and shoulders with effort. The only part of the body that is working hard, should be the pelvic floor, everything else including the neck, legs and head should be very relaxed.

Do not feel that you have to make this exercise deep or big. If it starts to get bigger automatically, follow it. There is no advantage in trying to strengthen the muscles in this exercise. If you feel pain in any way, you are doing too much. Relax and breathe the exercise rather than work it physically.

Section 1

Preparation: Stand with your feet comfortably apart with your arms hanging by the sides. Feel gravity pulling down on your shoulders.

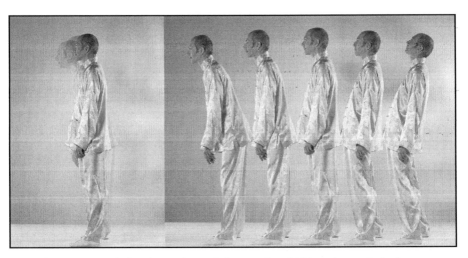

• Begin to rock backwards and forwards, shifting the weight between the heel and the ball of the foot.

• Bend the knees and feel as if you are going to sit back into a chair, breathing out. Then, squeeze the pelvis forward, breathing in.

• Again, sit back as if you're going to sit in a chair, breathing out. Continue alternating, sqeezing forward and sitting back, creating a small circle with the pelvis – breathing in and out as appropriate.

• Relax the head and shoulders and let the spine undulate, in response to the movement of the pelvis.

• As the pelvis moves forward the hands move back to meet the pelvis. As the pelvis moves back to sit, the hands move forward, away from the pelvis. In this way the hands create a circular movement.

• Allow the movement to get deeper by sitting back further – the circle created by the pelvis becomes an ellipse.

59

• Continue with the larger circles for as long as is comfortable.

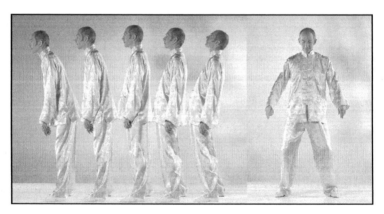

• Then, begin to make the circles smaller. And smaller. Until you are left rocking once again – this time the knees are bent.

Section 2.

• Raise the arms above the head, dropping the hands from the wrists – continue to breathe and rock. Wait here for as long as feels comfortable.

• Then, taking some time in each position, bring the palms of the hands to about 2 inches from the face, then the throat, the chest, the solar plexus, the belly button, the pubic bone. Then back up to the belly button, the solar plexus, the chest, the face…

• Finally, move the palms up to about 2 inches above the head.

Section 3

• Lay down on the floor, arms by the side, legs flat on the floor. Observe how you feel. Allow the breath to come and go, as it wants. Notice any different sensations but do not do anything about them. Allow yourself to completely let go.

• When you are ready, roll onto your right side.

• Push yourself up to a sitting position.

The Saint Making Medicine -
The Tranquility Technique

The sitting techniques for beginners – to regenerate and calm the mind.

The Saint Making Medicine – The Tranquillity Technique is said to take you to a place of silence. It also improves digestion and liver function.

This technique should leave you feeling calm and clear. Very good for busy people, or those with high stress lives.

It may take you into automatic meditation. Do not try to meditate. Instead, breathe and concentrate on the hands.

Preparation - Sit with the left wrist over right wrist.

• Breathe in. Move the right hand to the right side of the right knee.

• Breathe out. Move the right hand to the left side of the right knee. Drop the left hand onto the left thigh.

• Breath in. Move the right hand back to the right side of the knee, follow the fingertips to make a circle which ends where the thigh and hip meet. Slide the left hand to the knee.

• Breathing out. The right hand moves up the centre of the body. Turn the palm, resting in a half prayer position adjacent to the heart area. The left hand settles beneath the right hand in half prayer position.

• Wait here for a moment with no breath.

• Breathing in. Both hands move to the right.

• Breathing out. Both hands move to the left across front of the body in a big circle.

• Breathing in. Complete the circle. End with both hands on your right side. Wait here for a moment.

• Then, Breathing out. Slide the right wrist under the left wrist.

• Repeat on the left side, starting with the left hand.

Repeat on each side 36 times, or practice for about 15 - 20 minutes at your own relaxed pace. End by bringing the hands to rest on the knees (palms facing upward). Sit and observe how you feel.

You can also do this exercise sitting on a chair

The Loving Healing Turtle

The Loving Healing Turtle is a preparation exercise to 'heal' the heart. It is useful for depression and other emotional challenges. It is also excellent for the circulation and kidney energy.

Section 1

Preparation: sit cross-legged on a cushion on the floor, or on a chair with the feet flat on the floor. Rest the hands on the knees.

• Breathing in. Keeping both palms of the hands in contact with the body, slide hands up the thighs and the body to the heart area.

• Breathing out. Slide the right hand down the inside of the left arm.

• Breathing in. Slide the right hand up the outside of the left arm. Continue sliding the hand over the shoulder and back to the heart area.

Repeat on the other side:

• Breathing out. Slide the left hand down the inside of the right arm.

• Breathing in. Slide the left hand up the outside of the right arm.

• Continue sliding the hand over the shoulder and back to the heart area.

Continue

• Breathing out. Slide both hands down the body and the thighs to rest on the knees.

Section 2

• Breathing in. Slide the hands along the thighs, up the body to the heart area.

• Breathing out. Continue to slide the hands up along the neck and over the face to the top of the head.

• Breathing in. Slide the hands down the back of the head over the shoulders and behind you to hold the small of the back.

• Wait for a moment.

• Breathing out. Slide the hands over the buttocks down the thighs...
Uncross the legs, place the soles of the feet together and grab the toes
– Keep the breath out of the body.

NOTE: if you are sitting on a chair your hands will hold the knees; they
will not slide down to the feet.

• Holding the toes (or knees if on a chair) with both hands, gently pull away from the feet (or knees) and stretch the chin towards the sky.

• Keep the breath out, and let the body fall gently toward the toes.

• Breathing in. Slide the hands up along the inside of the legs and thighs. Continue sliding the hands up to the heart area while you cross the legs.

Continue alternating Section 1 and Section 2.

This exercise can also be done sitting in a chair.

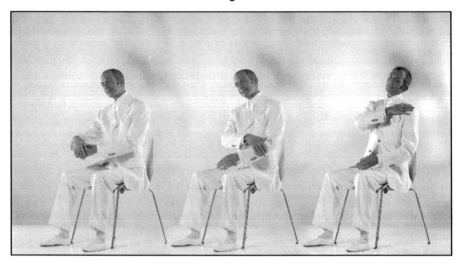

8. Signs of Success

We may notice signs of success that tell us the work we are doing is having an effect on the body, mind and spirit. These signs are noticed more intensely when we can relax more fully during the exercises:

- Heat, anywhere in the body, but particularly in the abdomen.
- Saliva in the mouth.
- Moisture on the skin.
- Moisture in the anus.

The standing exercises may leave you dripping with perspiration. This is to be encouraged.

Part Three: Practice

9. How to Practice

Traditionally, one should practice an hour twice a day. Not many people can fit that into their busy lives. Half an hour practice is good; fifteen minutes is good. If you have physical challenges or have a physically more mature body, start with five or ten minutes and let your time get a little longer as the weeks pass. If you cannot practice twice a day, practicing once a day is also excellent.

The amount of time you devote to the practice is not as important as being consistent. The exercises have a cumulative effect. That means that the results you get from them now will increase as you repeat them. Repetition on a regular basis is the best approach.

It is no good forcing your self to practice for an hour at a time - that type of conscious insistence on beating the clock is counter-productive. On the contrary, allow yourself to get carried away, letting yourself drift with the feeling of the movements, and continue for as long as feels good. Whereas there are no strict rules as to how long you should practice, there are guidelines that, as mature adults, we should be able to assimilate into our daily training sessions. Above all, you should be creative and spontaneous, allowing instinct to guide you.

We are more interested in observing the results of what we are doing, than achieving the perfect form of movement. Do not become obsessed with how you are performing, but rather, enjoy the moment and later observe how you feel.

One of my clients in Los Angeles was disturbed by feelings of paranoia. She started to come and see me every week. She began by learning the basic movements and found rapid results – in only two weeks, everything changed for her. Her life became very stable, her confidence returned, she was able to make sound and swift, yet difficult choices without the usual mind numbing confusion. After four months, we were still working on the basic moves.

One day she realized that most of the radical changes had come about in her state of mind, her body and lifestyle, before she had learned to perfect the moves. This was a huge revelation to her. Although I had repeatedly insisted that she not worry about the form, and instead concentrate on certain basic principles as I had demonstrated them to her, combined with a feeling of continually letting go, she had not really believed that that was what she should be doing. She thought I was being kind to her, not making demands, and patiently waiting for her to 'get it right'. On this special day, however, she suddenly understood what I had been trying to teach her about the work.

She remarked that it was an unparalleled experience. No

other undertaking shared this quality of not needing to get the form absolutely correct, and she had tried very many techniques. She estimated that when she had first been taught by me she had got the techniques about twenty percent correct. Nevertheless, she experienced positive results almost immediately. She wanted me to tell all my students of her experience, to encourage them to continue to work confidently with the technique, without discouraging themselves because of imperfect form. Having worked with me for many months now, my client also understood the value of sharing time with an expert, who understood the manifold depths of the technique. She recognized that each time I did a session with her, I was transmitting the technique to her, not so much through my words and demonstrations, but also through the subconscious messages I sent her. This was an accurate assessment of the dynamics of learning the technique efficiently. The master teacher conveys so much through subliminal communication, through pictures and feelings transmitted directly from one mind to another, whilst in the course of the session making energy adjustments in the student, which enable the work of the student to progress and reap benefits.

Hsin Tao does not seek to make experts and professionals. Those achievements can be realized through the martial arts, which readily encourage such goals. Instead, ours is a process designed to help people heal themselves.

We need to gain the transmission, then practice. We are not interested in perfection; we are only interested in results. Even getting it 'twenty percent right', when guided by a qualified teacher, will bear fruit. There is no need to strive or criticize yourself – only the need to practice regularly and let go – let the work work for you.

Try to practice in the morning. Morning practice will set your energy for the day. Experiment with different times. What suits one person may not suit another.

The movements will affect you differently according to your constitution. The first standing movement to regenerate the body, for example, will often give the practitioner lots of energy. On the other hand, if the constitution is systemically tired - that is fundamentally tired at a very deep level - the movement will make you want to sleep. Sometimes people start doing that exercise at night because it helps them get a good night's rest. After some weeks or months however, they might find it gives them energy to stay awake longer. In such a case, the practitioner would adjust the times of practice to suit their daily routine and the way they feel, and start doing the exercise in the mornings.

If you are having a very stressful time, it is advantageous to concentrate on the sitting exercises. The sitting exercises regenerate and calm the mind. If you have physical challenges, you should concentrate primarily on the standing exercises. The standing movements regenerate the body. Of course, the focus will change as your state of health changes, and rarely are our problems confined to physical or emotional. So a combination of standing and sitting is often appropriate.

In the initial months at least, one should practice no less

than one exercise from each section of the work – movements for body, standing up; movements for mind, sitting down; and breathing for spirit.

When you have become accustomed to all the exercises and have learned what they do for you, you can treat them like a kind of medicine chest, and chose the one that suits you for the day or week, or even time of day. For example, the seated exercises for the mind can be used even in the office. Once you have practiced for some time and built up the accumulated effect, even a few minutes will bring a powerful relaxation and clearing of the mind. In this case, if you are having a stressful day, close the office door for two minutes, sit in your office chair, and go through the movements to bring yourself to a state of calm clarity.

Try not to make a big deal out of practicing. It is helpful to practice in a quiet, clean space when you have time free. Traditionally practice was begun in the very early hours of the morning, when the pressing worries of the world seemed a little more distant. This however is not the rule. Be casual about practicing. The advantage of these exercises is that you need no special clothing, no special space or equipment. You can do them almost anywhere you can swing your arms. Try to take advantage of this lack of requirements, and allow yourself to practice spontaneously. When the thought strikes you, start to practice. See how long you can let yourself go with the flow. For example if you are at home, walking between the kitchen and the bedroom you suddenly think, "I should do some Hsin Tao

– the Saint Stretches His Waist" – then and there in the hallway begin your movement. You might only do it for five minutes as a sort of 'fill in' exercise session; or you may get carried away and spend twenty minutes or so transported into your spontaneous moving meditation. In this way, the work becomes more a part of your life. Avoid needing special circumstances and conditions, which may limit your ability to integrate the movements into your daily routine.

As I write, I have just implemented this very idea of spontaneous practice. Sitting so long at a desk in front of the computer, my back began to ache. In fact, one of the things I must still be careful of is not to sit in one position too long, stand still too long, or indeed walk for too long without a break. I have been at the computer for days, sitting still for hours on end, and my body has started to rebel. So the pain I experienced today was the accumulation of days of being too still. My body was becoming a bit like a stagnant pool, with not enough circulation and oxygen to keep the water clean. I thought I'd stand up for a moment and take a break. As soon as I took two steps away from the desk I thought I should do a little of the Saint Stretches His Waist. I began to undulate the spine and rotate the pelvis. Although I thought I might do this for only a few minutes to loosen my back, I found myself getting carried away, finding the right way to move so that I would not hurt my already tender back. Soon I felt myself wanting to incorporate other aspects of Hsin Tao, so I let it flow and followed my instincts. I forgot all about a five-minute interlude, being increasingly absorbed in what I was doing to relieve the pain in my back. When I felt I had done enough – there was ample heat and moisture to make me feel I had done a good workout – I lay myself down on the floor. The pressure on my lower back from the floor was quite strong, and I felt pain there, although it was not debilitating. So, I lay as long as I could and observed the pain. If it got too much to bear I would move. As I had expected the pain did not get worse. I felt my body let go in several places, pulled by the weight of gravity on the carpeted floor. I waited and observed, trying to let go as much as I could. After some time the pain began to subside. When it was almost completely gone, I allowed myself to move. As I stood up, I noticed that twenty-five minutes had passed as if it had been ten. I took two or three steps. There was no longer any pain. Instead, I experienced a strange feeling in the lower back where the pain had been, a feeling of intensified inner activity, but the pain had completely disappeared. I sat back down at the computer feeling refreshed and relaxed, pain free.

An eighty-year-old client in Austria uses this technique in a similar manner. She has for many years, suffered from worn out disks between the vertebrae of her spinal lumbar. She had found no relief until she started practicing Hsin Tao.

The seated exercises did not really appeal to her, because she found the hand movements were a bit confusing. Instead, she concentrated on the standing movements to regenerate the body. Within a couple of weeks, she noticed almost total relief in her back. The pain, however, comes back if she sits too long, stands for too long, or strains. Now, as soon as the pain returns, she does a short five to ten-minute practice, and the pain is instantly relieved. It is wonderful for her not to need painkillers any longer, and not to have to worry about her back. She reasons that it is age that has afflicted her spine, so the short ten-minute remedy she has devised using Hsin Tao is a perfect solution, one which she enjoys, gives her independence from being reliant on people or products, and also relieves the worry of future degeneration into pain. This one small instance of pain relief has brought with it not only peace of mind and but also enthusiasm for the future.

10. Consistency

The best way to approach Hsin Tao is by working regularly. Even if you do not achieve the full time frame of practice that you intend, it is advantageous to practice every day. It is like taking drops of medicine. Everyday, with each drop, the organism is prompted a little further into its own healing cycle.

An analogy is the way we push a swing. One big push every now and again will not provide the swing with its full momentum. To get the swing into a truly healthy and energetic rhythm we have to add a little push every time it returns to us. If we try to make the swing move in a huge arc with one great push, we need a lot of energy, a lot of movement, and the momentum quickly peters out. On the other hand, starting the swing in a small way with gentle regular pushes, and adding to its momentum each time it returns to us, little effort is needed, and very soon the swing is moving in a huge arc, swinging with more force than we used to give it a push. More than this, when the swing is in full momentum, you find that each time you give it another push you actually use the momentum the swing already carries with it. It has built its own momentum that makes our work easier.

So too, with the work of Hsin Tao: through gentle repetition on a regular basis, we start the momentum of the body, mind and spirit healing and regenerating itself. In time we discover that the organism has taken on its own momentum of change, be it fast or slow according to your own needs and native constitution. Practicing every day is like giving the swing another little push in the right direction.

In this way, we encourage the body to continue its process and its cycles of healing and regeneration. Don't feel you must unfailingly practice for long periods at a time. It is advantageous to do so but it is not the rule. The rule is to work within your own limits.

Practice to the extent that you feel involved. Go through the barriers of resistance, and observe what is happening rather than trying to do too much.

Avoid effort, mentally or physically. Above all, avoid pain. There is no advantage in working into pain.

Feel as if you are floating through the exercises, breathing and letting go. The less effort involved the more effective the work will be.

Utilize all these principles and work on a regular daily basis. Twice a day is better than once a day. Once a day is better than nonce a day.

11. Energy from Heaven

In Hsin Tao, we draw energy through the 'fourth eye' and send it down to the belly. This fourth eye, or Heavenly eye, is situated one inch above the third eye, in the middle of the forehead. Its sole function is to draw 'energy from heaven' into the body.

Traditionally, energy from heaven indicates energy from the heavenly realm of the Yellow Emperor. This is a sublime form of energy, which directs us into right action.

In our modern day approach, we substitute our own personal concepts for the traditional concept of energy from heaven. Whatever your image of divine perfection may be, use that concept as your energy from heaven. If you are a religious person and conceive of a "heaven", most certainly draw energy from this heaven and move it down to the abdomen. If your belief system cannot conceive of heaven but instead of a cosmic spiritual realm, then draw energy from this cosmos through the fourth eye.

There is no necessity for you to hold any such beliefs to proceed with this energy dynamic. Those people with beliefs in atheism should merely draw cosmic energy from the far reaches of the universe into the fourth eye. Buddhists who follow the deities and bodhisattvas can draw energy from an image of the highest god or bodhisattva. Hindus likewise can draw energy from their favorite heavenly image of god.

Energy from heaven is a particular form of energy. In fact, it is a sort of pre-energy. That is, it is not energy as we understand it, until it enters the body. It exists in the cosmos as a potential - the potential for all things that follow. Although we speak of it as a potential, it is not purely an imaginary substance. It actually exists as the potential for material energy, and as such presents a highly potent substance. Quantum physicists have discovered this same potential constituting a very real part of the universe. In Hsin Tao we utilize it to its fullest, ascribing it to the realm of 'heaven', and recognizing the unlimited source of this energy fuel. Being unlimited, we can draw from it every day, every minute, to increase our own store of bodily energy, whilst at the same time drawing into ourselves the cosmic instigator of 'right action'.

The decent of energy from the fourth eye to the abdomen, starts as imagination but becomes a very real feeling. With practice, it can become an ecstatic experience.

Energy from heaven is a direct connection to the source of our inner strength. Drawing on this energy is a natural function of the body, one that is pronounced in children. As we get older, we lose the ability to draw this energy down into the lower abdomen where it should add to our supply of stored energy. Reintroducing this dynamic is simply reminding the body of something it already knows how to do but, due to the natural ageing process, has forgotten.

Increasing our connection with this source of divine energy and adding to our own store of energy, we increase the body's defense mechanisms, inner strength, emotional equanimity, and bodily resilience. Drawing in heavenly energy through the fourth eye is of enormous benefit, even if no other aspect of Hsin Tao is practiced.

Many people ask what the difference is between the 'fourth eye' at the centre of the forehead, and the more commonly known 'third eye' situated between and slightly above the eyebrows. We receive divine love through the fourth eye. We project love through third eye. At an advanced stage of Hsin Tao, a feeling of ecstatic bliss can overtake the practitioner. This is the time when love can be most effectively projected to the world through the third eye.

12. The Ceiling Becomes the Floor

There are two signs of success when practicing Hsin Tao. The first is heat. You may feel heat anywhere in the body, but especially in the lower abdomen. This is not something we try to achieve. It is however a sign that the movements are having an effect. This heat, generated by slow gentle movement is very beneficial for the entire organism.

The next sign to look out for is moisture. First, you may experience saliva in the mouth. If you find yourself with a mouth full of saliva, swallow it – it is said to be very good saliva if it has been generated by these movements. You might also experience moisture on the skin in the form of perspiration. Perspiration generated by this slow, non-vigorous exercise tells us a number of things. Primarily, you are moving toxins from deep in the system. Secondly, the body is burning fat.

The final sign of lubrication to look out for is moisture in the anus. When we experience saliva, perspiration, and moisture in the anus, we know that the entire organism has started to manufacture its internal fluids. I call this moisturizing from the inside out.

The ultimate sign of moisture may take many years to be generated. This rare and wonderful experience is a taste of sweet nectar that drops from the upper palette onto the tongue. Such a sign means the body's essence has been transformed into healing ambrosia, which is circulating the body.

When you first start practicing it may take ten or even twenty minutes to start experiencing signs of success. Each individual experiences a different time frame when developing these positive results. The amount of time it takes to start feeling heat, which turns to perspiration, varies in each person according to his or her native constitution.

A person with a cold constitution might take weeks, even months to develop sufficient heat, whilst a person with a hot constitution may start to feel heat within minutes. As one ages, one's constitution may change. The core of the body cools down naturally as we age. Lifestyle can encourage this process. For example, if you have a male body and you have had a lot of sex in your life, you may have become very cool at the core. The opposite may be true of women. A reduced sex life in later years, which is the normal pattern, may encourage cooling - in which case you need to do something else to encourage that warmth and moisture to spark in the lower energy centre. Hsin Tao is the perfect practice for women to rekindle and maintain warmth without resorting to vigorous exercise, which promotes production of male hormone.

Hsin Tao movements have a cumulative effect. If it takes you ten minutes this week to generate heat, in a few weeks it might only take five minutes. So, we say your 'ceiling' becomes your 'floor'. That is, what you can achieve this week, becomes your starting point in weeks to come. Deepening and improving the work in this way is not achieved by effort or exertion. What is needed to continually make your 'ceiling ' your 'floor' is simply gentle repetition. Regular, relaxed and effortless training, brings about natural improvement.

If you want to experience more heat and moisture, you need to practice for longer periods and apply more relaxation. Try to let go more and more as you enjoy, rather than work at it. Above all, regular repetition brings results, according to your own constitution.

13. Mistakes

Many people, when first practicing Hsin Tao, think they are not getting it right. They believe that they have to get the form perfect. When judged in light of other techniques they feel they must really perfect it before they can see results. This is not right thinking. We judge the movements by the signs of success noted above. As long as you are not straining and hurting your self, you cannot be doing it wrong.

The rule is this: you can only make two mistakes when practicing Hsin Tao. The first mistake is to try too hard physically. The second is to try too hard mentally.

In the first instance, we must be careful not to try and achieve results. We must always be vigilant that we are not straining any part of ourselves. Above all, we must avoid pain absolutely. The aim of the movements is not to exercise the muscles or create stretch or flexibility. All these things happen automatically. If we work with these movements as if they were standard exercises focusing on muscle strength, flexibility, and dexterity, we will limit their affect. At all times we must be careful not to consider them as exercises per se. This is a self-healing and regenerative technique, not an exercise program. The possibilities of physical change inherent in these movements are, in my experience, far beyond the possibilities of a standard type of exercise. It is as if these movements are not so much physical as they are mental.

One of my clients refused to practice more than once a week, but he assiduously went over the movements in his mind, imagining on a daily basis that he was performing the movements with precise attention to detail. After three months of such a dilettante approach, he decided to take up running again, having done no vigorous exercise at all for five years. One evening after work, he decided to run seventeen blocks to the beach and seventeen blocks back again, through the haze of a Los Angeles summer. When he arrived back at his front door, he was startled to realize that he was not out of breath. The weekly practice of Hsin Tao, both physical and predominantly mental, had somehow made his body fit enough to run approximately six miles without tiring himself. He was very excited the next morning when he told me his story, citing it as proof that what I consider an incomplete practice regime, worked for him nevertheless. I don't recommend this style of practice, and certainly the general results this particular client garnered were limited. Nevertheless, he definitely enhanced his physical fitness. Constitutionally, he had the advantage of a hot constitution, so he needed less work to get to the first level of success. This may have worked for him, allowing him to do less physically, while he used his mind to do the rest.

Through my observations, it has become clear that the more relaxation one employs to practice, the more effects of success one experiences. Let go more, make less effort, and avoid pain at all costs.

If you are experiencing pain, you are trying too hard. Perhaps you need to make the movements very small. Find a way of avoiding the sore spot. When I was in the most severe phase of Post Polio Syndrome, I used to be struck with severe spasms that shot through my entire torso. They were so painful that I would fall to the floor, unable to move. It would take weeks, sometimes a couple of months before I could walk and sit normally again after one of these episodes. When I was first learning Hsin Tao, I was struck with one of those frequent debilitating spasms. Unwilling to stop practicing after seeing real and positive results occurring for me, I would stagger to my feet and begin to sway backward and forwards, and commence the Saint Stretches His Waist to regenerate the body. I would make the movement absolutely tiny so that it might have been hardly perceptible to an onlooker. Even though I could not walk without severe pain, I was able to make this movement combined with the breath, without causing myself any pain at all! I continued this for five or ten minutes, or until it felt as though I might any moment begin to strain. Then I would stop. I repeated this tiny painless movement two to three times a day, meanwhile being confined to bed. The first time I managed this regime, my recovery from the spasm was reduced from 5 weeks to 3 weeks.

With a huge sense of relief, I felt as if some miracle had occurred. In those days, I was used to experiencing spasms frequently, almost regularly. Every time I applied the technique in this painless way, the recovery time was further reduced. With time and my continued practice, the spasms came with less and less frequency. The severity of the spasms reduced month by month, and my recovery rate improved from weeks to days.

Pain is a sure sign of making too much effort. In our modern society, which tries so hard to achieve and endure, it is sometimes difficult to understand a system in which pain does not equal gain.

Another form of strain is mental stress. If one practices the movements with an attitude of self-criticism, one is inevitably creating a type of stress, which will diminish the effectiveness of the technique. One should maintain a kind of laissez-faire attitude, in which one is observing rather than striving. With such an attitude, one can observe deviations from the perfect form with a sense of interest rather than self-reproach. Gently finding ways to make the movements more harmonious and bring them closer to the form without actually striving to get it right can absorb one's mind. In this way, we can observe what we do, letting the body and breath flow in its own natural way.

I have repeatedly seen practitioners experience the removal of blockages within their energy flow, and in their ability to let go of mental stress, as they practice over time. As these obstructions are released, the form of their work improves effortlessly - inevitably.

It is as if the inability to perfect the movements is related directly to peoples' personal blocks and imbalances. You have to wait for time to take you through the process of clearing and rebalancing. Then you can observe yourself getting closer to a perfect form.

Equally, one should observe results, not try to achieve them. Don't hold to preconceived ideas of how the exercises work. Nor should you try to repeat the effects you have previously experienced. All these mental attitudes encourage effort.

Allow yourself a free flowing observation of what happens as a result of practicing. Monitor yourself throughout the day to gage any subtle variations in your energy level, in your pain level, or in your emotional outlook. Trying to achieve results often has the reverse affect, in which results previously experienced are reduced.

Results, like healing, come in waves. We must allow for the ups and downs that manifest in harmony with the body's own rhythms. The more we can put ourselves in an observing mode rather than a doing mode, the more effective our work will be.

Even trying to practice for the required time can constitute over effort and strain. Let yourself become involved with the movements, and be carried away by them.

Often one begins to go into a type of light trance state soon after starting the movements. If this happens, go with it. Allow the trance state to carry you away. This is the beginning of automatic meditation. In this state, time seems to disappear. Often I thought I'd practiced for only ten minutes, but when I opened my eyes, almost an hour had passed by. At other times, I had thought to be practicing for at least an hour, only to find that a mere ten minutes had elapsed.

If you have time restrictions, it is best to set up an alarm clock to warn you of the approaching end of your session. In this way, you can keep your mind off the clock, and let yourself drift with the movement and breath, enjoying the sensation. Thinking of time restrictions is just as stressful as trying to fill a predetermined time-period with movement.

It is hard to believe, and in a modern context highly unusual, to consider that all other apparent mistakes are not mistakes at all. Instead, too much physical effort or mental strain are the only real mistakes.

All traditional ideas about effort and gain are replaced by simple repetition. The most effective practice is done regularly on a daily basis. Gentle repetition brings success. It is a concept in opposition to the heavy work out twice a week. In the workout principle, one is destroying cells to achieve re-growth. With Hsin Tao, we are careful not to take ourselves into the realm of destroying muscle cells.

An experienced practitioner approaches the work with such a developed level of gentleness, that the internal muscle systems are activated. Our usual approach to exercise is to allow large groups of external muscles to support the internal musculature. This also happens in our daily activity, not just during dedicated exercise sessions. As the body ages, the reliance on external muscle groups promotes a weakening of the internal musculature. You notice that many elderly people attempt to support themselves exclusively from these external muscle groups, while their internal systems tend to sag and wilt from habitual weakness.

These internal muscle groups are constructed of many, sometimes tiny, muscles. Muscles as small as the tip of your little finger support the spine. Groups of these tiny muscles support other parts of the skeleton and the large muscle systems.

When a baby is strengthening itself, it does so by gentle and relaxed movement, thereby, strengthening the internal musculature. Later, the child begins to develop its external musculature. With age, we focus exclusively on the external groups to the detriment of the internal. Many older people will tell you they feel weak inside even if they have strong arms and legs. In such cases the spine begins to sag, the head shifts forward on a slanting neck, and the body seems to shrink in a type of internal collapse.

Moving in Hsin Tao cycles with extreme relaxation and no effort encourages the smaller muscles of the internal muscle system to strengthen. 'Pumping iron' does not work with these groups of smaller muscles. Only gentle repetition triggers them. As soon as we employ effort, we allow the external muscle groups to take over. Whenever the groups of large muscles take over, they allow weakness to develop inside us.

Relying more and more on the internal musculature, and strengthening the tiny muscles which are so often neglected, causes a different kind of strength to be experienced. It is a species of internal strength, which translates into the psychology of the practitioner.

Many people construct their personalities in a way that presents a strong external persona, protecting and supporting a vulnerable, sensitive internal nature. We can often observe a type of psychological 'hardness' in people who express themselves through this type of external strength. In such cases, the person's psychology is so involved in protecting the weaker inner self, that it sometimes develops unnecessarily tough behavioral patterns, which do not reflect the true nature of the person. This dynamic of an artificially strong exterior protecting a weak interior, directly reflects the physical dynamics of inner weakness, supported by external strength.

If we can strengthen the body at a very deep level, bringing fortitude to the small inner muscular systems that support the entire body, we begin to experience a new type of inner fortitude. A genuine strength, arising from our innermost self, that can be felt as a type of internal support. The psychological implication of such a new experience is that we can express a genuine inner strength to the world. We begin to lose the need of portraying a strong, often brutal exterior, and can instead present our true self to the world.

This psychological shift comes about because on an inner level we feel strong and secure. Inner strength implies a kind of confidence. It is an ability to express ourselves from deep inside, without fear of being hurt or exposing the vulnerable being at our core. To physically shift our strength in this way from outer to inner has implications at many levels of our being.

14. Pain Does Not Equal Gain!

One of the most important things to remember when practicing Hsin Tao is that pain does not equal gain. It actually does not matter how small your movements are, as long as they are tied in with the breath. It is very important that you do not move so much as to cause pain.

We are often so used to working with pain, especially if we have a chronic condition to start with, that a little twinge seems all right, and sometimes even feels like a good thing. With Hsin Tao, this is not the case. No pain is appropriate. If you feel even the slightest ache, you should adjust your movements to find a way around the pain. Even if you have to make your movement so tiny no one could see it - that is better than working into pain. If the movement gets bigger by itself - that is without you consciously trying to make it bigger - and if that increase in movement does not trigger the pain again, then that is perfectly correct. Go with it.

It is of paramount importance that you are as gentle with yourself as you can be. Always work beneath your limits.

As you work you will feel a point where ease becomes effort. When I say effort, I do not mean strain. Effort comes a long time before strain. It is the difference between a feeling of lightness, a sort of floating effortless feeling, and the feeling of having to work at it. This cross over point between ease and effort is your limit. Only you can tell where this limit is. Experiment to find at what point you cross your limit, then reduce your effort. It is an advantage to always work below your limit. Don't work to your limit, work below it. This is often a difficult thing to understand in our modern societies. We are trained from an early age to use all our resources, and to push beyond our limits. At the very least, we are expected to work to the limit of our capabilities. This is such a basic tenant of our social framework that it is a hard concept to overcome.

Even when we think we are using little effort we are still usually using all our resources, pushing ourselves to get the job done well, often sacrificing our own comfort to deliver. In many countries I have visited, this emphasis on working to your limit, and for successful people pushing beyond that limit, has been one of the most difficult concepts to undo in people's minds. It is not something that can be easily assimilated after a lifetime of working hard and using all one's resources.

The fact remains that the best results from the Hsin Tao techniques are not achieved by this dynamic of pushing one's self. No amount of convincing you intellectually will enable you to make your bodywork below its limits. It is something the body has to experience. Most of us have spent the major part of our lives learning what it feels like to work hard at things. The adult body understands what it feels like to be focused, to concentrate and make an effort to succeed, because it learnt these skills as a child. We now are asking the body to unlearn its methods of success, without sacrificing success in our daily lives. That takes time and practice, and can be a little frightening in the process.

Social conditioning also accounts for variations in our ability to physically let go and work beneath limits. On my travels, the most difficult culture I worked with on this score, were the Americans – high achievers, enthusiastic, intelligent and dedicated, they naturally resist what in normal parlance might be called laziness.

The easiest to convince that they could achieve more by trying less, were the Fins – used to long months of relative inactivity, good at waiting, easygoing, and able to concentrate without huge amounts of stimulus.

Between these two cultures were a variety of different aptitudes toward being able to quickly find a limit, and work below it.

In all our western societies, relaxation is equated with being inert, not moving, lying on the beach, perhaps watching some entertainment, or being massaged. Of course, there is the other form of so-called relaxation, which is sport-based, but this is really a type of stimulation to lift our spirits, and perhaps keep us fit. Rarely is true relaxation associated with movement and breathing. It is a shift in thinking and bodily experience, that once learned, may change the way we run our lives.

For all people, one of the most difficult aspects of Hsin Tao is to allow yourself not to go to your limit. Learn to feel that you are actually doing something well even though it does not cause any part of you pain, strain, or stress. It is an adjustment in thinking, which can be very rewarding. Find your limit, and work below it. You will probably find that you are much more productive, can do more, and the implications in your life may be far reaching.

The businessmen I have worked with, having discovered this ability in themselves, all commented that the influence on their business and private lives has been dramatic. Learning to work below their limits, they have told me, enables them to do more, be more creative, find more time in the day for work and pleasure, whilst their businesses became more productive, profitable, and enjoyable. Pushing past your limits reduces overall productivity and efficiency, and dramatically reduces long-term effectiveness. Think of yourself at work, when you are too tired to think efficiently. Problem solving and decision making often become a struggle. Even physical dexterity may be reduced. If we learn to stay below the limits, we remain at maximum efficiency. Burn out is another problem that arises from pushing past personal limits. Your emotional and mental reserves are taxed, until you feel frayed and exhausted. Staying below your limits reduces stress, and shows you how to handle pressure more effectively. When we do not habitually leap over the barrier of mental and emotional endurance, our stress tolerance, and capacity to withstand crises when they arise is increased. We allow our reserves to build, and develop a habit of feeling calm, which serves us in all situations.

Try to discover how much you can relax with the movements of Hsin Tao, how little effort you can put into it, and how much you can really let go. If you practice regularly, you may find yourself breaking through barriers of relaxation. The level of relaxation you are comfortable with now might not seem relaxed enough in weeks to come. You will realize that you can relax and let go even more. This may happen two or three times until you become comfortable with the level of real relaxation and ease in practice that is your true level of 'letting go'. Through this process, you uncover levels of relaxation within yourself that begin to apply to your every day life.

In my experience, the more you relax, the more pronounced the results become. The more pronounced the results, the more you want to maintain your relaxation and quiet of mind throughout the day.

One client from Switzerland, who was in her late fifties, came to me after months of practice. She had found that the work had stabilized her whole life. She felt centered relaxed and healthy for the first time in years. Over a period of a few weeks, she found that the magical feeling she had experienced throughout the previous months, the feelings of well being and stillness were no longer as strong as they used to be. She began to try harder, practicing for longer times, concentrating harder, trying to improve the movements. She even tried practicing two to three times a day. No matter how much effort she put into it, nothing seemed to work. Finally, she began to doubt whether the exercises actually worked in the long run, reasoning that perhaps they worked for her initially, but now they had done their work and would be no use any more. As this was the only activity in her life that had brought her back to a state of contentment, she was not at all happy at the prospect of the practice getting weaker. Her hopes of going deeper into the practice were almost dashed, even though more than anything she wanted to continue exploring this newly found feeling of well being that now pervaded her every day. Unhappily, she explained her situation to me. As I listened, it seemed that the mere desire to go deeper into the practice had undermined her. That craving to develop more of what had been started made her try to achieve. At first, it was not much extra effort, but her enthusiasm could not help but affect the way she practiced. When she found the effects becoming weaker, she tried a little more. As her concern grew, she tried even harder. At last, she gave up, all together frustrated, thinking she had done something wrong.

In fact, she had made the mistake of trying at all. Once she had arrived at a plateau of seeing the movements work with a cumulative effect every time she did them, she really needed to let go more. Not try to get better at it. Let go even of the idea of achieving any results. We spoke about this for a while, and as we did she realized she had been caught by her enthusiasm and had started to make effort during her sessions.

She began again with an affirmation that she was not going to try at all, and that she did not care what the results were, whether she experienced the cherished feeling to which she had become accustomed or not, did not matter. All that concerned her was that she kept up a regular practice. Even the amount of time she spent on the movements was no longer of any interest to her. With this attitude firmly in place, she instantly got her results.

Although she noticed the feelings return, she did not allow herself to become involved in them. Instead, she kept practicing trying to apply less and less effort. She simply observed, as if from a distance, the heat, the moisture, the feeling of meditative stillness that came over her. The focus was on letting go and moving from her centre - trying to make the movements and breath almost totally effort free.

Not only did the old feeling return, but she also notice two distinct differences. First, the effects of heat, moisture and peace, came faster than ever before. Second, and this was where she really had to use her concentration to relax more, the effects were stronger than ever before. Although she had previously thought she was relaxing, that former level of relaxation was no longer enough. She had taken herself to another level of the exercises, and instead of putting in more effort, she had to take effort out.

I explained that she might come to another impasse such as the one she had just experienced. It might be months away, or weeks away, or even years away. Whenever it came upon her she had to bear in mind to do the opposite of what we have been conditioned to do...try less, observe more, and allow the body and breath to lead.

I had experienced similar events. In my enthusiasm for the results, I had found myself trying when I didn't even know I was trying. It is hard to imagine just how little effort we need, especially as we become more expert. The level of effort I put into the work now would have seemed ridiculous when I first began to learn. Nevertheless, I went through at least three levels of having to let go. Each time I did, I experienced a profound increase in the cumulative, effortless, and pain free effects of the work.

15. Barriers

Because Hsin Tao works on all three levels at once (body, mind and spirit), the psychology of the practitioner is inevitably affected. Whilst encouraging change at such a deep level, we can also encounter barriers.

The first hurdle in any undertaking of this sort is to get yourself to practice! A part of you will insist that it does not want change. It wants to remain as it has always been, regardless of how uncomfortable that habitual inner dynamic has become. A voice will rise up within you expressing itself as lassitude. It will insist that you cannot be bothered moving your pelvis or your arms or sitting to breath for even a moment. Your habits will try to assert themselves, and rather than spending half an hour practicing Hsin Tao you would prefer to watch television for an hour and a half. These types of obstacles to practice constitute the first mental barrier.

The second barrier usually occurs after you start your practice session; at which time anything other than what you are doing becomes irresistibly important. If you recognize this mental distraction as merely a barrier, it will probably disappear within 30 seconds, and once again, you will be able to absorb yourself in what you are doing.

Ending your session at the barrier will create a pattern. I have timed a number of clients who have stopped unwittingly at the barrier. For all these clients, the barrier occurred at between 5 and 5 1/2 minutes after they commenced practicing. Having stopped at the barrier, each time the barrier subsequently arose it was at precisely the same time – between 5 and 5 1/2 minutes.

It is always best to let the barrier pass before ending the exercise. In this way, you allow yourself the opportunity of extending the practice into its own natural time phase.

Another type of barrier that I have worked with is boredom. One of my clients came to me after practicing for a couple of months, having achieved substantial results for herself. She complained that after all this time, she was beginning to develop boredom, and consequently the results and improvement she had been experiencing were not being sustained. I asked her what exactly boredom meant? After some self-searching, she was able to define the experience as wanting to think about something else, other than what she was doing. This desire to shift her attention away from focus on the exercise made her want to stop the exercise all together.

I inferred that at the root of this dynamic was a type of mental stress and mental effort. I suggested to her that she was trying too hard to focus her mind. "Yes" she replied, " I keep wanting to clear my mind and get myself into that clear relaxed state that I was experiencing before. I want to keep totally focused on the centre of the movement." I reasoned with her by asking how she felt at the end of the exercise. She affirmed that she felt calm, clear, relaxed, whilst her body felt as if it had done a complete workout. I explained to her that what happens during the exercise is not of paramount interest to us. Although a part of our attention should go into this process of movement and breath, it is the effect of what we are doing that is more interesting. How we feel after the exercise and throughout the day is more important than how calm our mind is during the exercise.

I suggested that she stop trying to be meditative during her practice sessions, and that she allow her mind to drift where it would, gently bringing it back to focus on the physicality of the moves, but not trying to exclude all other thought.

She came back to me after a week and with a broad smile exclaimed, "the boredom is gone! I was trying too hard to concentrate."

Instead of trying to focus intently, she began a more relaxed attitude to what she was doing. As a result, the exercise began to focus her, automatically. Throughout the process, thoughts and problems were thrown-up into her conscious mind. Sometimes the solutions to problems were flashed into consciousness. Trying to focus the mind like a Yogi and feel clear and meditative every time she practiced constituted too much effort for her, which over time had turned into a barrier.

Every person is different, and goes through a different process, experiencing diverse and individual results. We should allow ourselves to flow freely with whatever arises for us.

16. Cultural Differences

It has been my observation, as I have traveled the world teaching Hsin Tao, that there are cultural differences that come into play when approaching a new subject. Although Hsin Tao is perhaps the easiest exercise method I have ever encountered, on first learning, it can be confounding.

In essence, we are teaching the body a new language, and learning any new language takes time and application. It is no use learning the movements intellectually. The body must begin to understand. This physical memory relies on repetition and the passage of time.

It is like learning to walk; at first, it is a challenging process. You have to deliberately place one foot before another. Your balance has to be adjusted at every moment and there are many things to think about to save you from falling over. After some time, walking becomes so natural to you that you barely have to think about it again.

The movements of Hsin Tao are learned in the same way. It takes time and repetition for the body to understand and remember the movements. During this process, the mind is occupied with thinking of the many different aspects involved. One should not be discouraged by this initial phase of learning. After some time, depending on the individual, the movements will be absorbed into the body's memory. At this time, you might look back and wonder why you found any difficulty in learning these movements at all.

You realize that it is not the movements that are difficult; it is training the body that presents a challenge.

Training the body is like training any animal. It takes time, patience, and persistence. Once the body knows what you are trying to do with it, it responds ever more willingly. At this point, it becomes easy to go deeper into the exercises and discover ever more aspects to them. The body needs to understand the language of Hsin Tao first. Then, all else follows.

In every culture, I found a different reaction to this initial phase of learning. In the USA, people where so determined to learn, that they kept striving and pushing and using tension. The main challenge for me, as a teacher was to encourage them to stop striving, and allow the natural process to unfurl with all its imperfections.

In Finland, the students were so adept in concentration, relaxation and trust of the teacher, that they were able to overcome the barriers of initial awkwardness and move effortlessly into the Hsin Tao language. Each with their individual bodily interpretation of what was required.

The Dutch were busily enjoying themselves learning what they considered a new and exciting physical workout that could improve libido. My job in this instance was to bring them into a more subtle scrutiny of their own movements, encouraging them to give up effort and preconceived notions of what these movements could do for them.

In Britain, there was a stoic concentration on getting it right, and yet I needed to address a certain lack of confidence. Although their natural enthusiasm soon helped them conquer that problem.

In Germany, this lack of confidence was more prevalent than anywhere else I taught. On frequent occasions, I had to demonstrate to the participants how negative thoughts influence the outcome of any good works. The concept of a positive attitude was more important here than anywhere else. It helped overcome the hurdle of self-doubt, which manifested itself in repeated thoughts of: "I will never remember this, I will never master this." The solution to this particular problem was to consciously replace the negative thought with the positive " I will now remember this easily, I will master this with ease."

Cultural differences combined with personal differences formulate our own individual challenges when learning any new body language.

It takes a certain amount of determination to learn anything new, particularly as we get older. Since Hsin Tao is specifically for the more mature body, the issues of learning difficulties, self-confidence, and self-esteem inevitably arise during the initial learning period.

One should encourage oneself as one would encourage a child. Taking self-doubt lightly, being gentle and patient, allowing oneself time to learn; time to get it wrong, and time for it to come right. Enjoy the journey of learning and experiencing the effects of the undertaking.

17. Universality

Hsin Tao is a complete system in itself. You could successfully use it in place of other styles of exercise such as aerobics, stretching, moderate weights for muscle definition, Tai-Chi and traditional meditation techniques. In my observation, it effectively works on the muscular systems, as well as strengthening cartilage and connective tissue. It also tones and strengthens all the vital organs sometimes improving their function beyond the individual's metabolic norm. The middle ear's function is strengthened and exercised, noticeably enhancing balance in the individual. This is of particular use to the elderly. The skeleton can also benefit, joints can be strengthened and lubricated while the spine and posture can often be realigned. Brain function can be increased due to an increased flow of energy; breathing and sexual function are often enhanced.

Added to these physical benefits are enhancements of the mental and emotional faculties. In most practitioners, the mind is dramatically calmed, often within the first half hour of learning the technique. I have seen a number of cases where emotional instability, ranging from mild anxiety to clinical depression, has been eased.

Although it is a complete form of exercise itself, it can also be used as a highly affective augmentation to other techniques.

Many experienced meditators have noticed that working with Hsin Tao before their customary meditation enables them to go deeper and quicker into their usual daily practice. Some people have even commented that doing Hsin Tao before meditation, has led them to a more profound experience.

Often yoga practitioners notice that Hsin Tao gives them more stretch and flexibility whilst improving their balance throughout their yoga session. I remember two clients who were devotees of 'Power Yoga' – a particularly active and strenuous adaptation of yoga. I suggested to them that for the initial few weeks, they ease off their usual Power Yoga regime in order to observe the changes Hsin Tao might make within their bodies, minds and energy patterns. Both took a break for two weeks then went back to a power yoga session. One woman found a surprising improvement in her ability to keep up with the class. Her strength, flexibility and balance had taken a quantum leap. The other remarked excitedly that it was the first time in five years that a Power Yoga class had seemed easy, and she was able to maintain a relaxed attitude from the beginning to the end of the session.

There are many other instances where Hsin Tao has been used to augment and improve people's favorite practices and pass times.

A doctor in France, who had practiced Tai-Chi and Chi-Gong for twenty years, having trained with eminent masters of the technique, came to asses my teaching program. Within twenty-four hours of doing the beginner's workshop, he had discovered a new depth, breadth and stillness in his Tai-Chi/Chi-Gong practice. In that one day, he realized a new level of his work that he had not been able to obtain with twenty years of dedicated training.

It is up to the individual to discover how they will use Hsin Tao. The amount of time they put into it will reap its own rewards. One does not, however, have to abandon one's favorite exercise or meditation in order to adopt Hsin Tao into the daily routine.

In the initial months, one should allow space between the Hsin Tao practice and any other practice. This will enable the practitioner to take note of any changes that Hsin Tao initiates. This is only a suggestion, not the rule.

There are very few stringent rules in this technique. Once you have understood the essence communicated by a master, it is up to you to decide, how, when and where to practice.

In the Shaolin monastery before the Cultural Revolution, this technique was reserved for the most senior and experienced monks. There was no one to tell them when, why, or how to practice. This autonomy is one of the attractive aspects of the work, helping us discover that we need rely on others less, whilst uncovering more of our innate ability to take charge of our own lives.

18. Immortal Like the Gods

Hsin Tao is a self-healing technique. It is not just a series of keep fit exercises. If you practice Hsin Tao regularly, it may start you on a healing cycle. A natural healing cycle takes you through many changes. Some of these changes can be experienced as improvements, some feel like a downward spiral. If you follow the pattern of natural healing in it's organic process, making a graph of your progress, you will usually find a sort of wave pattern emerges. This wave is inclined on an upward spiral. That means that the 'highs' – the peaks of noticeable improvement in health - get higher, and the 'lows' – the troughs of apparent decline, or resurfacing of old symptoms - progressively become less low.

Overall, the spiral takes you upward. But you have to be prepared for challenges as the body readjusts itself, expels toxins at deeper and deeper levels, and replaces old discarded matter with new healthy growth. This part of the process can be physically uncomfortable, emotionally challenging, or even mentally confronting. It is important to go through these stages with a sense of confidence about the outcome. Be gentle with yourself, and keeping an eye on the positive overall changes that manifest.

Many times in my own healing cycle, just as I found myself getting better, I would experience the old symptoms again. At first, I felt a little discouraged. But when I looked at the situation logically, I realized that the returning symptom was less intense than the old symptoms used to be, and that they lasted for much shorter periods. Taking this as a positive sign, I used my own determination to keep practicing, even on the down days. Over time, I noticed this strategy enabled my body and mind to undergo huge changes that were surprising in their scope.

All natural healing occurs in cycles. Indeed the body, the earth, the solar system and the entire universe all operate according to cycles.

Even the life span of humans is considered by the ancients to occur in cycles. The first cycle of life lasts about 60 years. The following cycles are shorter, and we can measure their duration as we notice the changing patterns of day-to-day health. In our eighties, the cycles have shortened so much that we notice health changing on a daily basis.

This first sixty-year cycle is a great time to prepare for the oncoming deterioration of the body. If we are equipped with a regenerating technique, it is possible to slow down or even reverse the usual decline that people experience. Remember, Hsin Tao is not for maintaining health, but for regeneration. It can counter the process of degeneration we all experience. The possibility of a longer life span, or at least a more comfortable experience in the ageing body is possible, depending on how much time one puts into it and how expert one becomes before the end of the first cycle. That is why it is also called 'The Way of the Immortals'.

Every time a body changes its cell structure, adding or losing, or just replacing those cells that have died, it is no longer the same body. It has transmuted itself into a new body, defined by its new composition of cells. Hsin Tao encourages this transmutation process within the body. It can speed up the process of renewal at the cellular level, and at the deeper levels of mind.

For example, when the skin renews itself every seven years, it is a new skin. It has different characteristics from the previous skin, defined by its new composition. It may be thicker or thinner, dryer, smoother or rougher, colored in a slightly different way. We often think of this as ageing. But it is more than that. Over a cyclic change that has taken seven years to complete, we have grown a new skin. One that is characterized by the food we have eaten, the air we have breathed, the water we have imbibed or bathed in, and any number of other external and internal factors. The combination of all these influences, together with the natural cycle of regeneration and decline, have transmuted the skin into one that in many ways looks and behaves differently from our previous skin. Including a regenerative technique into our daily regimen will add a telling influence to the newly developed skin.

Using certain secret formula, the ancient Chinese Alchemists and Immortalists sought to metamorphose the physical body into one that could live for a much longer time. They wanted to transform natural physical ageing from a downward spiral into a self-sustaining and regenerating cycle. This meant that the nature of the body, and its tendency to decline after 30 years, would have to change. To achieve this, the alchemist needed to transmute the body's fundamental cellular patterns into a structure that could keep living 'forever'.

Alchemists the world over discovered that transmutation of physical matter also involved changes on other less gross levels. The mind and emotions were necessarily a part of such changes. Certainly, to achieve the desired transmutations the mind had to be very focused and calm. And the emotions were often raised to a level of exultation, ecstasy or bliss.

Hsin Tao is a type of internal alchemy that not only encourages a healing pattern, but in my experience also confers feelings such as ecstasy and bliss in a relatively short time. Remember though, that every person is different, and the time it takes will vary according to how cold and dry the body is to start with, or how fixed the mind is in its patterns.

Another factor in achieving fast results is diet. If we are trying to heal ourselves, it helps to ingest as pure foods and liquids as possible. Pure foods make it easier to experience ecstasy because the body is not so intensely involved in purifying whatever it has digested. My diet is strictly vegetarian, with minimal dairy and processed sugar.

When Buddha Bodhi came to the Shaolin Monastery, his Hsin Tao was absorbed easily into the Monastery's ideology, and has remained a part of the 'Immortality Techniques' ever since.

Many people may ask, "Why would you want to live longer

than is natural?" The answer has less to do with the body, and more to do with the mind and spirit.

A long life span provided more time, and therefore greater opportunity to develop a calm mind, and increase spirit. Calming the mind meant eradicating obstacles to inner freedom and peace. With a growing inner silence, an Immortal would be able to attune to the ecstatic limitless inner world, the true connected Self that was his divine source of life and love. By increasing the spirit, he was able to fill himself more and more with a 'spiritual light' - an essence of being, which is indescribable, yet craved by all of us. Usually, this true source of inner light seems impossible to find. Yet it is the cause of all internal happiness, and the quest to find it is the reason for all human life.

People are always trying to somehow find this inner peace and happiness. They come to me with all sorts of problems and reasons for their dissatisfaction, but it is always, basically due to the same cause. Mistakenly, we look to the external world to satisfy our craving. We think the new house, the car, the boy friend, or the new job will fill in this gap. But eventually, we all come to the same conclusion. None of these things brings lasting satisfaction. It is no secret. The joy from any satisfied craving is only temporary. After a while the boyfriend is more annoying than gratifying, the house becomes a burden, the car gets scratched or towed, the job takes over your life, and once again you are on the lookout for someone or something to make you shine, to bring you joy, satisfaction, inner peace. Looking for these in the external world is an endless merry-go-round, a big dipper of ups and downs that doesn't stop until we fall off the tracks.

By transmuting the body into a vehicle that lasts longer, we necessarily must transmute the mind and spirit as part of the process. That is the way alchemy works - any brand of alchemy - even this set of simple exercises aimed at inner transmutation. The immortality process helps us find more 'spiritual light' and inner peace. The more of this light and peace we accumulate, the more successful our lives will be. Certainly, within the system of belief based on transmigration of the soul (or re-incarnation), a life saturated with 'spiritual light' and deep inner peace is seen as a great plus. In any case, more spiritual-light feels better; it feels more comfortable, less stressful, and encourages our senses to be heightened.

In the immediate circumstances, the more spiritual light we hold, the more inner peace we have - the more inner peace, the greater the possibility of finding spiritual light. Once we are saturated with spiritual light, it automatically begins to spread to others. Spreading this light is one of the greatest contributions one can offer to humankind. It brings with it inner peace to those who accept it. To be of service in this way invites in even more spiritual light...and so the cycle continues.

19. Every Body is an Alchemist

The body is the ultimate alchemical laboratory. The changes that occur in the body minute by minute are considered by even mainstream researchers to be just short of miraculous. Although science can explain bodily functions through a mechanical approach, the underlying reason that this mechanism works is still a mystery. Scientists uncover increasingly complex and challenging possibilities. Many discoveries are controversial. Finally, the only core explanation is 'life', and that is still a subject of intense research and speculation.

Every moment, the body transmutes matter, turning it into something entirely different from what it started as. It turns the energy inherent in food into useable energy for the body, actually changing the biological constitution of the food into other forms of matter. The combination of food, air, water and energy, is transformed continually into living cells of many different kinds. The body is a transmutation factory extraordinaire.

Add the right ingredients, and the natural transmutation factor can be given direction.

Thought and right action act together to influence the body's health and happiness. Every thought, every deed, influence the body at a fundamental level, causing healing and harmony, or degeneration and disease. For example, many doctors recognize that a patient undergoing surgery has greater chances of survival if they maintain a positive attitude – i.e. positive thought patterns. Psychologists know that buried guilt can cause people to develop diseases of body or mind, not only due to the psychosomatic influence, but also as a result of chemical triggers in the brain that stem from feelings of guilt which themselves stimulate a complex web of reactions in the body. Acts of charity or good deeds on the other hand make a person feel good about themselves and encourage positive thought patterns.

The combination of these thought and deed ingredients are orchestrated, chosen, and administered by every individual. We are the rulers who combine these elements in the crucible of our own physical selves. And the choices we make directly influence how the body develops. These choices are important, not only in our formative years, but throughout our lives, well into 'old age'. We construct our own healing, or poisoning, formulae every day with a combination of food, thoughts, words, water, and activities. These ingredients change our physical structure, they influence our internal organs, and they cause the organism to regenerate, or degenerate.

All this takes place in the alchemist's laboratory we call the body, and each individual is the chief alchemist in charge of production.

Everybody is in fact an alchemist, running his or her own alchemical laboratory. Often we make mistakes when deciding how to run the lab. We end up in pain or anguish, with strange growths, or energy malfunctions; depressed, crippled, or bitter.

We cannot all be expert body-alchemists, so we rely on others who have a better idea about what is going on in this complicated and often challenging state we find ourselves in – the state of being physical. In fact, even the greatest experts often cannot help us. At best, they may solve our problems temporarily. But they rarely stop the chain of events that accompanies the physical decline we find ourselves in due to lifestyle, habits, or genetics.

As much as we may learn about the body, it is never enough. Even the best of doctors find themselves on the operating table, or relying on chemically derived medicines. There is a simple path that ordinary folk can follow, that eases the burden of disease and allows a healthy and enjoyable life to flourish. A way of working with the body that is uncomplicated, and does not take a genius I.Q. to master. Hsin Tao.

If the body is an Alchemy laboratory, it is a very special one indeed. In a normal lab, be it modern day chemistry or ancient alchemy, the mechanics of the lab, the experiments and the transformations that take place are due to the involvement of someone who works diligently inside the laboratory. That is, the involvement of a conscious human being. Where the body, as a chemical factory and transmutation laboratory, is so miraculously different, is in its inherent consciousness.

We often tend to treat the body as an unconscious factory. A sort of lab that has no mind of its own. We often cannot hear the body's demands for different food, thoughts or activities – or if we do recognize these needs, we often chose to ignore them until it is too late. Since we treat the body as a type of factory/machine, we rely on the mechanic or the scientist to adjust it, tune it up, put it right. We lay the burden of responsibility in other's hands - frequently with disastrous results.

The body is indeed a factory, but it is utterly conscious. In fact, each individual cell has its own consciousness. Every organ has an awareness of its own. For example, the cells of the heart work together, vibrating in the same rhythm to establish the heart's pumping action. If you separate those cells, even if they are on opposite sides of a room, they will still 'pump' in a perfectly synchronized rhythm. In other words, each heart cell shares a consciousness of when to pump and when to relax – and they will continue this action in unison, for as long as they remain alive.

Each organ actually talks to every other organ. Only when the organs are in conscious cooperation and act as a part of a whole, will the organic function of the body be harmonious. It is not unusual for a particular organ to start doing its 'own thing', and have to be persuaded into working in harmony with its brother and sister organs.

The language of the organs is one of impulse, or raw energy transmission. Organs signal each other with this raw energy in much the same way as we speak to each other with our voices, or signal to each other with our hands and eyes. By channeling energy along its natural pathways (what the Chinese call Chi), we can encourage a flow of communication between organs, or stimulate the flow of energy to a particular organ, thereby persuading it to perform its specialist function whilst communicating in a harmonious way. Such harmony between the organs brings about a state, which we describe as 'good health'.

Since the body is inherently conscious, we don't need to be expert scientists, acupuncturists, or alchemists to run it successfully. To a very large degree, the body takes care of itself. It utilizes its own consciousness to act as its own healer. If we treat it as a conscious entity, we can steer it in the right direction, whilst letting it be its own captain. This is exactly the way Hsin Tao works. It fills in the gaps and helps the body find its own equilibrium.

Given the right ingredients, the body knows exactly what to do to maintain good health, or even to improve health and increase the life span. All we have to do is wake up the body's inherent self-regenerating mechanisms – and begin to respond to the messages it gives us. The rest is automatic.

20. Heat, Moisture, Tantra

If one were to categorize Hsin Tao in terms of yoga or martial arts, it would fall under the title of Tantra.

Tantra traditionally focuses on raising the fundamental energies that lie dormant in the body, or more accurately become dormant as the ageing process advances. This reawakening of previously dormant energies is regarded as being a cornerstone to a type of higher awareness, as well as being an avenue toward better physical and psychological health.

Although the moves are reminiscent of different forms of martial arts, this is not one of them. Being a type of 'Tantra', it may be classified as yoga – it may be called Zen Buddhist Yoga. The essential meaning of 'yoga' is 'union', indicating a union of the individual with the absolute divine; or rather, an experience of that 'union' which already exists in every being but is as yet unrecognized.

Unlike other forms of Tantra, Hsin Tao does not seek to force energy to rise or move. It encourages such movements and awakenings through a natural process, similar to the processes that occur in growing children.

Children store an enormous amount of energy in the lower abdomen. The result is that they are warm and moist. The lower abdomen should be the warmest part of the body. When there is an excess of energy in this area, energy begins to circulate throughout the body and many pockets of energy stagnation begin to move with the tide - as part of a natural, gentle and safe process. With Hsin Tao, one never forces energy. If it begins to move by itself, we encourage it by introducing specific moves. Otherwise, we wait for the body to find its own way bring about change.

If you watch a baby breathe, it uses the abdomen as a bellows. The belly works to bring breath in and out of the body, whilst the rest of the body and limbs are completely relaxed. The motivation for the breath comes from deep down in the lower abdominal muscles. As we get older, our breath becomes more and more shallow. Teenagers usually breathe from the base of the ribs. In our twenties, the seat of the breath moves to the middle of the rib cage. Finally, in old age people find themselves breathing from the very top of the chest in short shallow bursts. Our connection with the energies and motivating feelings deep in the belly, just above the pubic bone, is lost by degrees, without any conscious awareness that such a process is taking place.

Two things accompany this process. First, the abdomen begins to cool down. People begin to experience symptoms that indicate cooling. Symptoms like constipation, urinary tract and bladder problems, reproductive organ problems. The list continues, but any symptom occurring in this area is usually telling us we are cooling down at our core. As the problem continues, the cooling spreads. After some more cooling, people experience cold hands and feet, and general intolerance of cold. The cooling factor also depends on the physical constitution with which we are born, the passage of time, and our connection with the original seat of breath – the lower abdomen.

The second thing that occurs as the seat of breath moves further up the body is that the body begins to feel dry. Hair, nails, skin, joints, mouth and lips, all become dryer. Huge industries have evolved around the re-lubrication of an ageing body. Physical aging, even in very healthy people, is to a large degree associated with experiences of drying and cooling.

I was always sensitive to cold weather. As I grew older, I found myself becoming intolerant to cold. My hands and feet would ache with cold even on a warm day. After a few years practicing Hsin Tao I found a dramatic difference in my ability to stay warm. Although I still prefer a warm climate, my hands and feet stay much warmer, and my core body temperature remains more even. I am able to withstand cold situations much better, and rarely is being cold any longer a trigger for coming down with flu. The practice has increased my body's ability to maintain its own warmth, and has provided a more stable core temperature closer to what I experienced as a child.

Only last week a homoeopath in London commented on the moisturizing effects of His Tao. She told me that within the past few months she had stopped practicing for a period of four or five days. On the last day she realized that she felt much less well than she had become used to after months of regular practice. What most impressed her was that after just three days without practice her facial skin began to dry out. She had noticed her skin looking better since she had begun to practice, but it was only now that she realized just how dramatic the effect was. In the days she had stopped training, as she looked closely in the mirror, her skin began to look pasty and scaly. It absorbed almost twice as much moisturizer as she had become used to applying. Within one day of recommencing practice, the skin reverted to a moister appearance and absorbed less moisturizer.

The moisturizing and heating effects of Hsin Tao can be lasting, whether practice is maintained or not. A woman from London with osteoarthritis (a cold, dry condition) had wonderful results in the first months of practice. She felt so much better, that she began to shirk her practice. Inevitably, after months without training, she had gone considerably backward. The pain had come back, with the old weakness and severe restrictions of movement. Nevertheless she had not declined to her original state of debility. When she first came to a general workshop she was unable to place her two wrists together because of pain in her arms, elbows and wrists. With the first month of practice, she found, among the many dramatic improvements, that her wrists came together with natural ease. Now, although symptoms had returned due to no practice, she was still able to place her wrists together in order to perform the 'Saint Preparing Medicine'. Some of the changes Hsin Tao had caused in her appeared to be permanent, confirming my own experience. If she had not stopped who knows how many other changes may have become permanent improvements. The contrast in her condition catalyzed her into practicing regularly, and last I saw her she told of a complete and unforeseen change in physical, mental and emotional wellbeing.

When the breath is seated comfortably, and effortlessly in the lower abdomen, many people experience sensations of increased core heat, as well as moisture. Feelings of increased moisture are directly experienced on the skin as perspiration, in the mouth as saliva, and in the genital and anal orifices as lubrication. Hsin Tao movements make this happen automatically, subject to the time frame dictated by your own native constitution and physical condition.

The heat and moisture generated, combined with the extreme relaxation that often accompanies the work are signs that the body and mind's natural healing processes have been triggered.

21. Healing Patterns

Hsin Tao is not just an exercise program. It is a self-healing and regenerative technique. As such, it can initiate a deep healing process. This depends on how often one repeats the movements. If one uses the technique once or twice a week, it will probably only benefit in the way most exercise programs help to tone and strengthen, although there will possibly be the added advantage of mental relaxation. When the work is repeated daily – optimum is to practice twice a day – it can trigger the body's natural healing mechanisms. When the body is encouraged to heal itself, it must follow its own native pattern of healing.

A natural healing process has its ups, and downs. Following the natural rhythms and tides of the body, one can experience alternating improvement, and decline. As the body expels toxins and strengthens itself, it uncovers deeper layers of disease and attempts to throw them off. These periods of throwing off toxins can be uncomfortable.

This relates to a basic concept in Homeopathy, in which the organism is healed by a process of uncovering old symptoms, healing them, and going by stages deeper into the layers of disease, until finally the root cause of the illness is uncovered and brought to a state of balance. The idea being that merely curing the symptom is not going to cure the cause of disease. If the organism is treated symptomatically, the cause of the disease often remains even though the symptoms disappear. Since the basic disturbance has not been removed, the body will usually go on to develop another seemingly unrelated symptom. When the new symptom is treated, the cause that remains will throw up another symptom, and so it may continue year after year. Not only does the untreated cause continue to manifest new symptoms, but through neglect it often grows more virulent.

An analogy to this process of curing symptoms, which I call 'Fix and Hide', is the way computer systems develop corruptions and eventually break down all together, until finally they have to be taken to the computer wizard for resurrection. With symptoms of the computer slowing down, or not behaving just right, a quick fix, or a restart, will often temporarily fix the problem. Computers have an amazing capacity for compensating when part of the system is not functioning at one hundred percent efficiency. The quick fix however only serves to hide the real cause of the problem. While the computer continues to work, be it ever so slightly less well than it did the week before, it is easy to forget that there might be confusion or corruption somewhere deep in the system. What the computer really needs is an efficient diagnostic and repair program to check every detail, down to the deepest level of the system. If we don't do the deep repair and continue with the quick fix, the computer will continue to compensate until it has used all the avenues and compensations available to it, and finally it just can't do it any longer. The computer freezes, or refuses to start, and you have to go to the experts to get a deep and thorough repair job, which consumes precious time and money. All the quick fixes have only made the cause of the problem hide deeper and deeper in the system, making it harder to find and more difficult to resolve.

The body follows a similar process of compensation. Quick solutions only make the real cause of disease dive deeper into the system, while more complications and malfunctions keep surfacing, confusing us with strange and often apparently unrelated symptoms. Finally, the whole system breaks down in a kind of overload. It can't compensate any longer and suddenly serious help is required. Often we think the terminal illness or the need for surgical intervention has just come upon us out of nowhere. But frequently the cause can be traced back to years of lifestyle or diet, for example, which have been abusive to the body's delicately balanced systems. Digestive aids, or headache pills, or any number of quick fixes covers the abuse, whilst the real cause persists. Finally when surgery is suggested, the years of dietary mistakes might be regretted, but too late. The delicate chemistry of the body has been upset, and no amount of compensation has been able to bring the system back into balance. Enter the surgeon's knife.

The homeopathic principle stresses a basic need to uncover layer upon layer of symptomatic disease, until the real cause of disease surfaces. When the initial and true catalyst of illness becomes apparent, it can finally be treated. That process might take years, and often the symptoms that arise throughout the process are old symptoms that actually occur in a reverse order to their original sequence. So, whatever order in which the symptoms were originally experienced over the years, that order would be reversed as the organism starts to heal. As old symptoms arise and clear, the body is removing layer after layer of 'fix and hide' syndrome, until the original cause of disease can be brought into a state of harmony.

The computer and the body are both concerned with balancing their systems. A certain amount of juggling to maintain balance can be sustained. Finally, when balance has been completely lost, the unit as a whole begins to fall over.

During the natural healing process, the body's attempt at creating balance is constantly being readjusted. As one aspect of the imbalance is healed, the body begins to feel well again. Being in a state of temporary balance enables lingering causes of potential imbalance to rise to the surface. The new symptom is then balanced with the entire body mechanism, and the process continues. Healing, uncovering, healing, uncovering, while as a whole the body is getting stronger and more systemically sound. It gains such a state of stability and strength that it can afford to displace and reveal deeper, more fundamentally disturbing causes of imbalance.

This process is reminiscent of a pendulum, swinging back and forth, past a neutral point. Each time the swing passes centre, the mechanism is in balance, but soon swings out again past the central point. As the pendulum swings, its movements away from the central point become shorter and shorter. Eventually, the swinging action loses its momentum, and balance is achieved.

During this process, we experience periods of feeling very well – the 'ups', then periods of decline – the 'downs'. If the healing process is working effectively, we should experience the 'ups' getting higher, whilst the 'downs' get less and less deep. This process applies equally to physical and emotional recovery.

In nature, all things follow cycles. To remain in harmony with those natural tides, we must expect our healing to follow its cyclical pattern of 'ups' and 'downs'. Just as the sea has high and low tide every day, season, and year, so too the body follows cosmic laws of tidal activity.

One client I mentioned earlier was a great example of this up and down healing cycle. He came to me with severe nerve pain in his arm and had been living in a state of agony for about two years. After the first session with me, he noticed an improvement. Feeling better, he went to do some of his beloved yoga. The following day his symptoms returned. After our next session, the pain went away again. This time the pain free period lasted a few days longer. Encouraged, he played his customary game of tennis. The following day his symptoms returned. The cycle kept repeating itself. Each time he came to see me, it was easier to find the key to make the pain vanish and with every week, the pain free period lasted longer. However, we could never achieve a full month pain free.

One evening he came to see me after having had a treatment from a body therapist and he was suffering the worst agony that

I had yet seen. We sat together working on the problem, and frankly I thought that the method might have failed him, so severe was this recurrence that he struggled not to break down. By the end of the session, we had quieted the pain once again, but he was still in a very delicate state. He left with strict instructions of how to practice.

The pain continued to diminish after he left me. At the next session, the pain had not returned and I advised a certain treatment to relieve pressure in his skull. He followed my advice. The pain did not return. Finally, after weeks of experiencing his body swinging back and forth in its effort to heal this potentially operable problem, he found relief for a full month. He continued to be pain free.

It was interesting to observe that the 'ups' and 'downs' he experienced were not only associated with his body and personal health, but also with his lifestyle, habits and attitudes. He had to let go of some things to which he had become accustomed. None of that was difficult. The offending habits, thoughts and indulgences were left behind without any of the usual withdrawal symptoms. I have observed this often in people who practice regularly.

Most interesting was the pattern the healing cycles took. He followed the conventional pattern in which his pain free periods were getting longer, whilst the painful periods were shorter and less severe. Before his final breakthrough however, he experienced a huge climax of pain. This too is familiar to Homoeopathic theory. Before the major release of toxins, the body experiences a climax of the negative symptom – a catharsis before the final clearing. My client's bravery, perseverance and confidence in the method he had chosen to heal himself, were a major factor in his ability to get through the catharsis. (He might tell you that he had tried every other avenue available, and so was faced with no choice but to hope the Hsin Tao would work for him. Nevertheless, his innate qualities and clarity of mind in a crisis were huge assets that contributed to his success.) Thankfully, well over a year later, he is still pain free, with increased stress tolerance, and increased virility.

Experiencing the cycle of improvement might not be so dramatic. In my own body, I noticed many small changes occurring over the years. Small pains sometimes accompanied these changes. The pains of change had a special quality that I began to recognize as being quite different from the pain of damage to the body. They would not be constant, coming and going throughout the day, and most noticeably, they were not debilitating in any way. Sometimes at the end of the exercise session, when I would lay down on the floor, I felt small pains moving from one area of the body to another. Over time, I realized that these pains were actually a hallmark of changes in my bodily structure. I had for many years suffered from a curvature of the spine (scoliosis) between my shoulder blades. The influence of this problem kept my neck in constant need of attention and my lower back was always painfully compensating for the twist that stemmed from between the shoulder blades. One week, I noticed my shoulder was sore. Then the soreness left that shoulder and moved to the other. Following this, my knee became sensitive for about a week. When that disappeared, a pain appeared in my hip. The journey of pain continued from one place to another, but it was never too uncomfortable, nor did it restrict my movement, or ability to function. I would simply continue to practice, being very careful not to work into the pain, satisfying myself with small easy movements. One day, after some months of this process, I realized that my spine between the shoulder blades, had straightened. For some months the scoliosis would disappear, then return, but rarely was it ever as pronounced as it had once been. The times when it returned became shorter, whilst the periods of being straight were growing longer, developing into many months of being effortlessly aligned. After two years, it straightened permanently.

By degrees, the entire skeleton seemed to readjust itself. The most dramatic change happened over a year and a half after I began to practice.

The only real deformity I had sustained from the original bout with polio was a right heel that did not sit absolutely straight under the foot. It was positioned a little to the left, causing many problems and pains throughout my life. My right thigh ripped once from exertion combined with the heel's misalignment, and I developed severe tendonitis in the foot a number of times because of the stress caused by this same problem. I had tried so many different techniques in an attempt to straighten it, from yoga, to chiropractic and osteopathy, to many months of physiotherapy including ultrasound and straps. Nothing had shifted the wayward heel.

After practicing for some time, I had come to distinguish the pain of readjustment from the pain of damage. So, as I practiced one day and began to feel a sharp pain in my right ankle, I thought little of it, other than being careful to avoid the pain and not exacerbate it with my movements. When I finished my practice, the pain disappeared. This pain came and went throughout the days that followed; sometimes it would come while I was practicing, sometimes not. It followed all the usual patterns of a beneficial pain, but it was sharper than any I had felt before; and yet it did not interfere with my movement. I continued and thought little of it.

After six weeks of experiencing this pain at the same intensity, I began to wonder if in fact I had actually damaged myself. The many pains I had experienced in Hsin Tao were never as sharp, nor did they last as long as this. I reached down to inspect my ankle. It all seemed quite normal. There was no pain to the touch, no swelling or bruising. Then I noticed that my heel was sitting straight, aligned correctly. The curvature that made it protrude to the left had disappeared. I had to look over and again, just to make sure I wasn't imagining things. This was the first time I had seen my right heel sit straight! It was an exciting and revelatory moment. I was struck by the possibilities. What other unseen and virtually impossible changes could this Hsin Tao manifest, seemingly with a logic and action of its own, almost independent of my intention?

I realized that this pain in the ankle had been part of the Hsin Tao process that was now readjusting the position of my heel.

Since it was a very old problem and fundamental to the alignment of the entire skeleton, it was taking a while to resolve itself, and was a painful process. Overjoyed to see such a positive shift, I was happy to let my ankle hurt as much as it wanted. I continued to practice carefully, and following the precepts I had developed with Hsin Tao, made sure I did not irritate any sensitive areas with my movements, avoiding pain altogether. In another three weeks, I realized I had forgotten about the pain in my right ankle. It had disappeared sometime, without attracting my attention, leaving behind a straight ankle. I now walk with a straight heel under my right foot for the first time since I was five years old. My right thigh has become much more resilient, and my foot is much stronger and more comfortable.

Of course, I've also witnessed quite dramatic shifts in the body's alignment that came about without pain. Such changes can emerge with a degree of subtlety that they almost defy detection. One client in Los Angeles, aged about forty-one years, did not notice a dramatic change until after the event.

We were sitting together working on a more advanced breathing technique. My client remarked that over the past eight months, sitting cross-legged had become more comfortable for him. When he first started seeing me, he could work on the floor for only very short periods at a time. He had to do most of the seated exercises in a chair if he wanted to practice for extended periods. As time had gone by however, he was able to practice on the floor, seated on a cushion, for longer and longer periods, and so he had progressively less need of recourse to a chair.

He began to tell me about the problem of his bowlegs, and how that condition had, since childhood, limited his ability to sit with crossed legs. He had been teased about his legs since youth, and it was not only an unfortunate disfigurement physically, but had also left psychological associations – he identified himself as a bowlegged person – indeed his childhood nickname reflected this condition.

I had not seen this client for approximately six months, and did not notice his bowlegs when he walked into my LA clinic. I asked him to stand and show me his legs. With a little embarrassment, he stood to display his bowlegs. I could not see any pronounced curvature. Since he was wearing baggy shorts, I asked him to pull the shorts tight around his thighs to give me a better look. Try as I did, I still could not see any thing other than a slight curve, not in any way a bowlegged problem. He bent over to have a look at his own legs, whilst drawing the shorts tighter in order to get a better view. In consternation, he continued to inspect his legs. He shifted his feet here and there, trying to get the legs to bow out. There was no doubt about it, his thighs met, the knees were almost flush, whilst the calves were slightly apart, and the ankles sat perfectly. I asked if that slight curvature was what he meant by a bowlegged problem. "No" he said, "They were really bowed before. I guess they must have got better." He looked up bemused, then laughed happily.

He had practiced daily for eight months, all the while noticing that sitting on the floor was become easier than ever before in his life. Because he was so accustomed to the thought of having incurable bowlegs, it had never occurred to him that he might inspect his legs for change. Now, he was astonished that his legs had improved, without any effort, or intention. He had experienced no pain, nor any other symptom of his body realigning itself, other than the growing ease with which he could sit cross-legged on the floor. Primarily he had considered these exercises calmed his mind, and gave him greater strength and insight into his life. Having a healthy constitution, with no acute illnesses, he had no need to scrutinize the depth of physical change that was occurring. Nor had he even dreamt that such a fundamental change could occur under any but the most rigorous circumstances – and perhaps not even then.

His practice of Hsin Tao had produced dramatic change without the slightest discomfort. In fact, as I have witnessed so many times, the change was not even noticed until after the event, because it came about with such subtlety, and in perfect harmony with the body's natural equilibrium.

With more than his usual optimism, he drove straight home to inspect himself in the mirror.

22. Exploring Your Own Well Being

One of the three facets of Hsin Tao is 'rejuvenating and calming the mind'.

We experience mind every waking moment as a series of thoughts. Often there are so many thoughts that we are unable to rest. Sometimes thoughts make us tense or unhappy. If we try to stop our thoughts, it becomes obvious that it is not easy to make them go away. They will repeat themselves over and again, until they obsess us. Disturbing thoughts will wake us from our sleep, 'drive us to drink', distract us from our duties, and make life thoroughly unpleasant.

Our understanding of the world depends on the way we string our thoughts together. It is thought after thought that construct our world - be they accurate, false, confused, obsessive, peaceful, or fearful.

We usually find it difficult to hold a single thought for any length of time. It has been said that to hold a thought is like tethering an elephant with a piece of string. It simply won't stay where it is put. It breaks away and develops into other thoughts, other pathways and new directions. If we somehow manage to hold a thought, other thoughts quickly come in to barrage us and distract us from, or add to the original thought.

Overall, our day is comprised of thousands of thoughts, layer upon layer. To find peace of mind we have to slow the thought process down, or at least find a place of quiet among the barrage of thoughts - a respite of stillness in the midst of this internal commotion.

The many single thoughts, joined together at lightening speed, in their various and often fascinating layers, are like pieces in a puzzle that combine into a seemingly endless, continual stream of conscious awareness.

On the other hand, when the mind slows down and thoughts are not so virulent, we automatically experience inner silence. When the silence is experienced for longer and longer periods, the mind becomes tranquil. When tranquility is experienced for extended times, the mind transmutes itself from constant activity to bliss. This is the theory behind Hsin Tao that I first heard with a large amount of skepticism. Through practice, I began to realize this dynamic of slowing the mind into silence actually can be achieved through repetition of the simple Hsin Tao work. It was not some mystical and unattainable formula – the proverbial carrot that would tempt me to apply myself. Instead this was a state I was able to experience in a relatively short period of time, without even trying to focus the mind! The first time I experienced a silent mind I realized that in all my years of so called meditation I had been fooling myself. I had actually been doing mind expanding / creative imagination / concentration exercises. The mind had been actively involved in the play of peaceful meditation. Certainly many of these exercises had made me feel spaced out, or harmonious, or at ease, but all of these effects were quite dramatically different from the experience of a quiet mind. Although I thought I had experienced the real thing, once silence actually came to be it was almost with a dramatic thud. I could not describe this state, other than knowing effortlessly that this was the beginning of silence. Thoughts, if they arose, floated by like gossamer ribbons on a vast expanse. And all the time I was breathing and moving my arms in the sacred patterns of Hsin Tao. This dynamic did grow to ecstasy and then bliss, but I suspect that is as much the Grace of God as it is the practice of Hsin Tao.

It is not only thoughts that constitute the mind. Emotions make up a large percentage of our experience in the world. We often feel our thoughts with emotions. These associated emotions give greater impact to our thoughts, and inspire more thoughts and feelings. Thoughts, together with emotions, are a primary factor in our experience of being alive. They can be very useful to us, but as is most often the case in these fast, intense times, they drive us to illness - both physical and mental. Thoughts and emotions that cannot be contained may lead us to stress, depression, hopelessness, confusion, anger, obsession, resentment and hate. During the Post Polio Syndrome decline I experienced the entire range of these thought /emotion combinations and tried to combat and balance them with a thousand techniques. Only when I started making these relatively simple Hsin Tao movements did the mind, for long stretches at a time, finally give up and the emotions started to truly heal, without effort, and with permanent change.

The body is sensitive to our thoughts and emotions. Emotional impacts can actually affect the way the body looks – the way the body grows older. We can diagnose habitual anger in a person by a formation of certain lines on their face. A person who worries will form certain facial features that are common to all people who worry. Similarly, a person who smiles a lot and feels happy will form lines on their face that tell us they've been happy over and again.

The body responds to emotional impacts not only by the development of facial lines. Emotions felt intensely over a long period can influence posture, flexibility, dryness or lubrication, and general health. In general, thoughts and emotions largely influence the way our bodies age. Emotional impacts create patterns that fix themselves into the aging process – they might lend us vigor and optimism, or encourage us to become 'couch potatoes', or grumpy old men.

The body is alive and responsive to all of our input, whether we are positive in our approach to life or negative, whether we harbor resentment or anger, or whether we give freely of ourselves; all these varied emotional extremes are processed and assimilated by the body's unseen ability to transmute one type of energy into another.

The finely tuned and subtle variations of the Hsin Tao moves are specifically designed to re-pattern and support this hidden level of the body's nature. The flexibility of the style – without insistence on rigid perfection of physical technique – allows the movements to mould themselves to each individual's physical makeup. So, at the most personal and impressionable level of the body's consciousness, the subtlety of the moves can trigger change, releasing old wounds, increasing confidence; whilst at the same time accessing and opening channels of communication between the mind and body.

As the work integrates itself into the body, the mind becomes more sensitive to the body's needs and energy patterns. When this happens you are able to respond with greater awareness to messages the body sends up to the conscious mind. Triggering the body through Hsin Tao's subliminal body-healing keys stimulates an intuitive understanding of what the body needs to feel well, and makes it easier to respond. The changes in the body influence the mind by making the mind calmer and more receptive to its needs; and the changes in the mind influence the body by feeding it positive messages, substances and activities.

There are many techniques designed to make us feel healthy, relaxed and calm, but very few have been designed as regenerative techniques. Necessarily this means the work of Hsin Tao, if exploited to its fullest, will delve deeper into all the systems that create and support the physical body. This deep penetration into the mysterious systems of the physical frame can cause change at a fundamental level. With this fundamental change, we can expect to experience deep shifts of body awareness, emotional patterning and mental integration.

Although the moves are simple, the approach to them is more

complex than meets the eye. It is only after years of training that the practitioner begins to understand the complex interweaving - the multitude of factors that cause disease to be transmuted into good health, and further into a healthier state of physical and mental constitution. Thankfully, the genius of these movements enables us to utilize them without complex knowledge - as long as we receive them from one whose insight and understanding can guide us, with subliminal and overt messages, through the intricate tangle of interdependent systems – physical, mental, emotional, spiritual – that constitute our journey to better health.

Among the remarkable and difficult to explain phenomena that contribute to the body's everyday activity, is the breath. Just as the heart beats without being asked to do so, so the body keeps breathing.

The rhythm of the breath reflects not just the body's need to imbibe oxygen and expel impurities; it also indicates the emotional and mental states of the person. Breath is body's initial contact with the world at large. To work with the breath is to work with the primary influence that sets off a superb and almost endless chain of events at every moment. It is our connection to the universal rhythm, and to the spirit of life.

Spirit is the essence of the human organism. There are a number of facets of spirit. First, is the exoteric aspect, which we all experience as a life force within. It is the feeling of being alive. From a more esoteric point of view, our spirit exists almost independently on another plane, and imbues the physical presence with life whilst remaining a thing of 'another world'. The more spirit is connected to the body, the more alive we feel. When spirit leaves, we die.

The presence of spirit is manifested physically as 'essential fluid' or stored energy within the body. Young children have much of this essential fluid, which bubbles away in them as stored energy. They easily transmute this essence into hormone and chi,[5] which circulates throughout the body and gives them what appears to be almost unlimited energy. As we grow older, the amount of spirit or stored energy within the body is diminished.

With less stored energy, we lack the basic material to produce chi, so we lose vitality. The organs do not receive their much-needed nourishment of energy, and perform with less vigor.

Breath is our connection, through which we can draw spirit back into the body. All we need are some keys that will enable even the most frail among us to increase their store of energy.

The treasure of Hsin Tao contains a number of these secret keys preserved in their original form – as they were before being developed into the martial arts of Shaolin. They are keys that the body understands even if the intellect does not. When the body understands, it can draw from its own almost unlimited resource, to bring itself into balance and reverse the damage it had previously undergone through ageing or injury.

Spirit is also our ability to feel connected to our own true self. When we increase the amount of spirit in the body we become calmer, happier and full of energy. If we are calm for long enough, something happens to the brain, and calmness becomes permanent. When we are calmer, we can solve problems more easily – we know what to do, and can more easily see the path of right action clearly before us, we can experience a kind of wholeness of being – a type of self-satisfaction that does not rely on external circumstances.

Spirit fundamentally reinforces the entire organism. It relates to the mind and the body, because it invests both with the fundamentals of being alive. The entire universe is imbued with spirit. Our ability to draw that spirit into our physical experience is key to well being.

The human organism is a complex miracle. It is able to sustain a state of perfect balance in the midst of the greatest abuse. I believe it should be treasured and cared for, not in an external or shallow way, but with deep reverence as one of the miracles of the universe. Hsin Tao, in my experience, is equal to the body's greatest mysteries and miracles. Here we find a form of self healing held in reverence for hundreds of years, which, when handled correctly, can tap the body's potentials, taking them to the highest possible levels of transmutation, healing and perfection.

23. Re-patterning

We all experience the physical effects of emotions. When we are upset or angry, we often feel a physical response in the solar plexus region of the body. You can actually feel anger rise up the body before it explodes. Deep emotional impacts can result in the stomach becoming tense and digestion turning acid. If this kind of assault on the digestive system persists, more severe problems can develop, such as hiatus hernia, in which a 'nervous stomach' loses its ability to keep acids from flowing up the esophagus, a particularly uncomfortable and often painful chronic state. Repeated emotional challenges can cause wide ranging and lasting physical side effects. Loss of appetite, or overeating, lack of concentration, heart problems, muscle tension and headaches are just some of the symptoms that can be a direct result of emotional impacts. In a worst-case scenario, the nervous system can completely collapse, and we experience a nervous breakdown. Long-term emotional impacts can have long-term effects on the body, which actually influence the way we age.

Emotional impacts on the body not only derive from anger and stress. Many of us experience unpleasant or even frightening events as children or teenagers, when the mind is particularly susceptible to outside influences. Most often, these events are not articulated, but are instead submerged beneath conscious memory. These emotional challenges impact the way the teenager or child develops into an adult, in both psychological and physical aspects. Indeed the entire personality and body can be affected for life by early emotional impacts that have not been processed or resolved by the conscious adult mind.

For example, we all know that a teenager with low self-esteem will round their shoulders, almost as if they are trying to hide from the world. This psychological/postural shortcoming, will affect the teenager's general posture. With ageing, the postural shortcoming becomes a postural problem. That postural problem may develop into chronic back pain, frozen muscles, or various associated degenerative symptoms. This degeneration has been triggered by an incorrect skeletal alignment, which itself was the result of a self-esteem problem. That self-esteem problem could itself have developed from an emotional reaction to something so simple as a negative comment about a pubescent teenager's body weight, genital development, skin color, or any number of psychologically sensitive factors. The teenager, lacking clear insight into their complex state of physical/emotional development, submerges the emotional problem, expressing it as rounded shoulders, and soon loses all memory of what triggered the feelings of self-loathing. All that can finally be remembered is an unaccountable, and often, vague feeling of being less than good enough.

This close association between the emotions and bodily development is a type of 'patterning' - ways in which old emotions 'sit' in the physical body and influence our lives on a daily basis. These patterns direct our every day physical interaction with the world. Frequently they remain part of the subconscious content of the mind. As they continue to lodge in the unconscious, they exert an unseen influence, which can rule us, often into old age.

The patterns we develop through childhood, puberty, through our teens and into our adult lives, can compound themselves into a cage of physical reactions, which cause disease and discomfort. Many psychological processes have been developed to unlock these patterns and relieve patients of many distressing symptoms. Schools of somatic psychology seek to 're-pattern', that is to create a new pattern of emotional/psychological interaction with the body. This process often takes years to succeed, and leads the patient through a complex revelation of submerged emotions and motives.

This relationship between submerged emotions and the body's aging process is a powerful one. Like all habits, these patterns are difficult to uncover and change. They are particularly difficult to shift because they are anchored in the subconscious. From here, they can exert an undetected influence, causing us to believe that these patterns are in fact ourselves, whereas they are only patterns of emotional behavior we have adopted.

So too, as the body ages, we associate its patterns of deterioration with our true selves, as an inevitable consequence of our physical constitution. In many cases, these patterns of deterioration are a consequence of our internal emotional and psychological patterning. If we can change the emotional/

psychological patterns, we can often free ourselves of bodily patterns that cause discomfort, and distress.

Working with a number of Integrated Body Psychotherapists in California, we discovered that the Hsin Tao techniques appear to re-pattern whilst automatically processing the subconscious causes of physical discomfort. In the modern Shaolin Monastery, as directed by the Chinese Communist Government, some of these moves are still used to balance the emotions and relieve martial artists of problematic inner dynamics, such as anger, depression and discontent.

Re-patterning is, once again, a natural process of healing. As the re-patterning uncovers submerged hurt, depression, anger, or resentment, a period of adjustment may be needed. If you continue to practice through the adjustment period, the emotional impact of whatever is being uncovered is often greatly reduced, because the technique helps to process the buried disturbance that has arisen. At a certain stage, the emotions arrive permanently at a more balanced and resilient state, and the work of internal growth can continue without huge emotional swings taking place.

To heal the body successfully, we must heal the mind, which incorporates thoughts and emotions. No system works independently of any other within the human form. Body, mind, and spirit, must interact in harmony for all systems to function to their fullest capability. A union of these different elements can bring all the organs, emotions and thought processes into harmony, thus prolonging life and increasing bodily comfort. Why should we put up with painful bodies and distressed minds in our modern, sophisticated world, when we have the opportunity to use ancient non-intrusive methods to bring ourselves back into harmony? Why should we always seek the help of others, when we could first use our own energy and activity to promote better health, before overburdening professionals with problems that may well have been avoided, or even reversed by using a little sacred movement?

24. Self Sufficiency

Two of my clients have a combination of Lupus and Fibromyalgia. Lupus is an autoimmune disease that often comes in tandem with Fibromyalgia, which is an affliction of the nervous system. Decline, slowed by heavy medication is the prognosis for both diseases. Both clients had a long history of relying on doctors and medication. In fact, to a large degree, they felt completely reliant on the practitioners who treated them on a regular basis.

Exercise only exhausted them, so efforts to keep fit were difficult, if not impossible. Dietary changes frequently caused problems, because bloating, food sensitivity and digestive disorders accompany this combination of diseases. Any slip up in their regime, or even a change in the weather causes what doctors term a 'Flare' – a flare up of symptoms that leave the patient debilitated and often depressed. Sleep for these people is difficult without medication; and waking in the morning is often just as difficult as was getting to sleep.

Both clients came to me at different times, and both had difficulty with co-ordination when I showed them the exercises. There were, however, a number of positive results that came to both clients. Each chose exercises that suited them best. They practiced sporadically, but on a weekly basis. Both complained that everything else they had tried had triggered 'flares' and exhausted them, whilst now they were able to practice Hsin Tao without any negative side effects. Almost immediately, they both started to feel calmer.

Over the following year, one client found Hsin Tao stopped her decline, in spite of the medical prognosis. Even though she did not see dramatic improvement in her disease symptoms, she did find peace and optimism through being able to do something for herself. The results were modest, but that was an improvement on everything else she had tried, and finally she felt she could work with her doctor instead of relying on him for all her needs. With independence came optimism, which itself engendered a new enthusiasm for life. Both these attitudes, in a chronically ill person, are like panaceas.

The other maintained the exercises because she found they kept her calm, whilst at the same time easing her pain. She had practiced Tai Chi, Chi Gong and yoga, and being a psychologist had a wide knowledge of options when it came to panic attacks and depression – nevertheless, until practicing Hsin Tao, she could find no relief from these attacks, apart from medication.

The most dramatic improvement was associated with her 'flares'. She found that after a year of not so regular practice, they were less dramatic and passed away quicker than she could ever remember. Her ability to withstand emotional stress had improved, and she was discovering an inner peace that she described as her "heart opening".

Both women came and told me independently that the most appealing thing about the Hsin Tao work was a feeling of independence. Suddenly they did not feel reliant on other people. They could do something for themselves, by themselves, in their own time and place, when it suited them.

This feeling of independence gave both women the spirit to continue. Previously, they had both been discouraged by the difficulties of continuing their day-to-day lives, in such a desperate and painful situation. Now they felt they had something that could help, even if it was only to bring them into a state of calm. What interested me, regardless of the different results they had gained from working with the technique, was this idea of feeling independent.

They could both feel Hsin Tao working for them, and they could do it themselves, without having to get it perfect, without practicing for long hours, exhausting, or frustrating themselves. There was no need to buy special equipment or be in a special place. The sense of independence spilled over to other areas of their lives and both women would tell me of growing interests in other aspects of self healing, and arts.

If the only thing that Hsin Tao did were to give these women a sense of independence, confidence in themselves and hope for the future, it would be a great practice. At a time in their lives when nothing other than heavy medication brought any relief, the idea that a set of movements and breath could calm them, give them strength and a positive attitude, was like a miracle in itself.

Certainly, I had shared that experience when challenged with the depths of Post Polio Syndrome. From feeling helpless, and a victim of the disease, I suddenly had a tool that I could use without hurting myself. The freedom and optimism this engendered were amazing to experience. Couple this with the fact that I felt real and ongoing results, was liberating to say the least.

Self-reliance brings with it unforeseen possibilities. Beyond all reason, health can improve when all the odds are stacked against us. It has happened hundreds of times throughout history, which is peppered with what we call the miraculous. Why should we not, in the modern world, be able to share in these improbable possibilities of self-healing, inner peace, and a heart opening to love? At the very least we should be able to help our doctors heal us, and no longer feel frightened and victimized by disease, instead we should learn to trigger the natural healing powers of the body, and by so doing discover the almost super human inner resources of being human.

Self-reliance does not only mean independently nurturing your health. It also implies becoming less reliant on many of the props of modern day life. We know that stimulants like coffee, alcohol, cigarettes, or even marijuana are to varying degrees habit forming. We can tell ourselves a million times that we don't need these things and we should stop or at least cut down. To actually stop, to break established habits, whether one is physically addicted or not, can be surprisingly challenging.

I have observed a number of instances where habits just

drop away after practicing Hsin Tao continually for many months. Practitioners can become independent of the need to rely on outside stimulus, not because of any conscious effort, but simply because they feel better in themselves. The changes experienced are so subtle, people often they don't realize they have 'given up' until after the habit has been left far behind.

I have had feedback from people about forgetting to smoke cigarettes or drink coffee. One man told me that he only remembered he had not drunk coffee after abstaining for a week. He had simply forgotten about it. It was only then he realized he had neglected to continue with his daily regime. One week went by and he hadn't even noticed that he wanted water instead of coffee. He had just ordered what he felt like. His energy levels were higher than normal, and he had experienced no symptoms of withdrawals, such as irritability, headaches or tiredness.

The same has been reported with Marijuana smokers. They simply forgot to smoke. Cigarettes, probably the most difficult of all addictions to give up, have also been reported to me to be left behind without any withdrawal symptoms at all. I suspect that one particular cigarette smoker had it in her mind to stop smoking in the first place. Nevertheless, the ease and speed with which she was able to achieve a smoke-free environment surprised even her.

A client came to see me only last week with a story of how his diet had completely changed. It was not that he had intended to eat more healthfully. He explained that his taste buds simply did not want the food he was used to eating. Over a period of a couple of months, he recognized that he wanted mostly raw foods. By the time I had returned to see him in America he had an entirely new regime of eating habits. He had been practicing regularly every day for eight months, and was describing how he had observed changes in almost every aspect of his life. He was able to run his teams of employees with less strain, he was able to give himself more time off, he had slowed down, but found himself to be more productive, and most surprising to him, he had changed his diet. All this he observed in retrospect. He had not undertaken to do any of these things. His employees had first made him aware of the changes, by making small appreciative comments. It was only then he assessed the new habits he had unconsciously adopted. He now finds 'junk-food' tasteless and repugnant, whereas when I first worked with him, he had no problem consuming a daily allowance of the perennial American fast food and snacks, coupled with large daily helpings of red meat. His taste buds had changed his mind, and he tells me that he now feels healthier and calmer than ever before, with increased stress tolerance in the workplace.

These effects are not seen in everyone, but for those who need it, if they practice with consistency, a balancing of habits comes about that gives them more self-reliance and independence. Instead of needing cigarettes, alcohol, coffee, marijuana, or junk food to get through the day, many people find all they need is good food and water. They begin to grasp, on a fundamental level, that happiness and contentment do not come from stimulants. These qualities come from within.

Although we can understand this intellectually, it is the body that must really learn to understand. The body itself must begin to know that it feels better eating pure food, breathing fresh air and drinking pure water. We can tell ourselves a million times, but we usually face a battle convincing the body to obey. Overwhelmingly the body wins out in the end.

When the body wants to change habits, it can do so easily. It will then inform the intellect that this is what is happening – this is what it wants. Happily, we can observe a sort of automatic change take place, which makes us feel better and causes us no grief in the transition.

I have observed Hsin Tao quietly achieve this in a number of people. It seems to free them from the bonds of habitual behavior, and reliance on external stimulants.

The price they pay is the time they must allocate to practicing. If they work regularly and gently, interesting changes can take place that make them more their own person, freeing them from dependence and feelings of helplessness. Such a positive change has wide implications on every aspect of daily life.

We put enormous effort into our work, our children, our cars and homes. Some of that effort could readily be diverted to our own inner well being.

Hsin Tao, for many cases, provides such a vehicle for self help, independence, and positive action. It can help us change built up emotional patterning, and shift ingrained habits. Through gentle repetition, the possibility is available to almost everyone to become independent and free of past inner restrictions.

25. Running Water Does Not Rot

All life is movement. In fact, absolutely nothing is still in this world. Even if something appears to be still, in fact it is not.

On the smallest, sub-microscopic level, everything is made of tiny particles that are dancing and swirling around each other, forming larger particles, which we can detect as atoms. These atoms themselves dance and vibrate. They swirl in and out of what we see as matter. They fill the space between everything that appears to be solid. This atomic and subatomic movement pervades and underlies absolutely everything. It creates the basis of what worshippers of Shiva, the ancient Hindu god, refer to as the cosmic dance.

This 'cosmic dance' extends from sub-atomic particles, to the internal organs of all creatures, out through the solar system, and even further, to the farthest reaches of the universe.

The rhythm and movement of this cosmic dance is continually in a state of perfect harmony. There is a precise relationship between everything that moves in the universe, whether it is impulses of the heart, or the birth of a super-nova. We can picture this more clearly by imagining the universe to be a huge lake. Any movement in any part of the water causes currents and waves. The waves affect the air above the lake and cause winds to move. The winds in turn have an effect on the surface of the lake and create more waves. Every current or wave causes more water to be displaced, which in turn causes further currents. These new currents displace more water and cause new currents. So it continues in an endless domino effect. Every movement, no matter how small is related to every other movement within the lake. Whether at the surface of the water, or in the deepest depths, every movement of the water can be felt because of the current it generates.

Movement is the natural state of all things. To be still is to be dead. Even when one stands still, it is only an illusion. Physiologically, to keep the body still requires the involvement of many muscles. They work against gravity and against each other, in an attempt to keep the body still.

Even when sitting slumped in a chair we are not really still. Tiny movements of the muscles conspire to give us this illusion of stillness. Often we can lounge around with no apparent movement, yet still remain tense. In fact being 'still' or motionless for too long can build patterns of tension. We use so many counter-movements within the musculature to remain motionless, that it is often tiring. How many people complain that they cannot relax, or that they wake up with aches and pains? Being still is often hard work. No matter how hard we try to remain perfectly still the body will fundamentally not co-operate – it needs to keep moving to breathe and pump blood.

The fact that a constant movement is the natural state of all things, gives us a key to healthful living. In a natural state, all beings are engaged in a lot of movement. We call this exercise. Wild animals are generally healthier than domestic pets. This is primarily because animals in the wild have to work their bodies hard for survival - whilst domestic pets spend much time lounging around the house! Like their owners, they lead a largely sedentary life. That is, they do not move very much when compared to their counterparts in the wild. They instead spend a lot of time sitting, or lying down.

An old Chinese proverb begins, "Running water does not rot..." We all know water in a fast moving stream stays fresh. Pools of water, on the other hand, stagnate. Because nothing is motionless, the water in stagnant pools does not remain unchanged. It must respond to the laws of movement. Even a still pool of water is a part of the 'cosmic dance'. Left long enough, it begins to create a life of its own, filled with all sorts of bacteria and other moving life forms, causing degeneration of the water. This degeneration is 'stagnation'. It is a process, not a state of motionlessness.

If we want our bodies to remain at optimum health, we have to follow the universal law, and keep moving. We need not only to exercise our arms, legs, and external muscle groups, but also our internal organs, our skeletal structure, particularly the spine, our middle ear, and most essentially, the mind.

In Eastern philosophy the body is essentially energy. This is corroborated by modern physics. All things are essentially energy. This energy moves from one life form into another.

Before scientists were invented, the alchemists' told us that energy transmutes itself from one form into another. The energy in plants becomes the energy of the human body via our digestive tract; the energy of sun and water becomes the energy of the plants through the processes of photosynthesis and osmosis and so on. Physics now affirms alchemical thought, telling us that energy cannot be destroyed. It moves, instead, from one life form to another.

If the body is indeed primarily energy, we must keep that energy moving if we are to stay healthy. Otherwise, the energy will act like the pool of stagnant water and degenerate, fostering bacteria and life forms alien to a healthy organism.

So essentially, exercise is not wholly to do with moving the body. We must also get the energy inside the body moving and circulating. For exercise to be highly effective, we must move energy that fills every part of the body, including inside the internal organs, inside the spinal column, and inside the bones. It must behave like running water, maintaining its clarity and purity, strength and vigor, in order to avoid stagnation.

Running water does not rot, flowing energy does not grow old.

26. Advanced Hsin Tao Practice

What has been presented in this book is only the beginning of the Hsin Tao practice, although, even if this is all the practitioner learns, the potential benefits and changes can be enormous. It is not absolutely necessary to go any further into the technique, but the possibilities go far beyond the bounds of this book. The human mind being what it is, always seeks further stimulation to keep interest and involvement, so for those who seek greater depth, there is plenty of stimulation to draw them further into the practice.

There are various stages of advanced practice, each based on an assimilation of previous work. Before going to the next level, it is necessary for the body to understand the movements. This is only achieved by training the body through repetition. Once the physical form understands the beginner's set of exercises, one can refine and move on to the next level of work. All up, there are four stages of advanced work, until finally one is introduced to the central form of Hsin Tao. This is a twenty minute sequence performed sitting down, which incorporates all the energy dynamics of the previous exercises, (standing and sitting). This final stage of Hsin Tao brings insight into all aspects of life.

There are a number of signposts along the way when making progress with Hsin Tao training. None of these stages can really be explained. They must be experienced, and then the experience is described to the teacher who verifies it as an authentic gateway to usher in further, more advanced aspects of the work. The first signpost is the "circulation of energy" and "hot hands". The second is described as "seeing the golden light". Then you "come face to face with your own Spirit". Another is "producing nectar". The last is "going out".

It is always advisable to work with a qualified teacher if attempting to follow the technique into its deepest aspects. Much can be transferred only by oral and energetic transmission.

As deep as one may go with the technique, it is always based on simple repetitive movements – the one exception being the central and final technique, which is a detailed series of moves in the seated position. The standing exercises branch out into three directions. (In this book the basis of the first direction has been illustrated.) The advanced moves elaborate on these directions, maintaining a central circular theme.

When we go to the advanced levels, not only healing takes place, but also a certain ecstatic awareness begins to open within the practitioner. Innate talents are activated, as well as hidden potentials. One begins to crave peace and find it lasting throughout the day. There is an unlocking of the underlying and more profound aspects of being human. It is as if the walls of the damn are busted open and potentials are realized.

In my experience and according to the testimonies of others, it is not only the inner life that changes, but external circumstances also rearrange themselves to provide a more harmonious and nourishing set of worldly circumstances. Every person that has worked with me individually and has practiced consistently twice a day has reported a similar dynamic. Not only have their internal lives, physically, mentally and emotionally, improved, but the circumstances of their world have also realigned themselves to bring about a transformation. Their work might be more harmonious, or even different. Relationships at home may rearrange themselves in a positive way, financial circumstances may improve, friends may change – the picture often presented is a total move into harmony and balance, more in keeping with the authentic urges of the practitioner.

In the advanced stages of the technique, insight is possibly the greatest gift these exercises deliver. Insight into the nature of one's self and of the world.

Of course, all these benefits are latent in all people everywhere. All we need is the key to unlock them – to allow ourselves to be our true selves. It is not everyone's choice to take the practice to it's extreme. Hsin Tao can be used simply to bring about improvement and start a healing process within the human organism. If one wishes to continue to explore the depths and train to the levels of the immortals, this too is possible.

The more we train, the stiller the mind becomes. The stiller the mind becomes, the clearer is our understanding of ourselves. When we are still and clear, we can hold more spiritual-light. With an excess of spiritual-light we can heal not only ourselves, but also those around us. In this way, the precious gem of Hsin Tao can radiate its sacred light throughout the world.

May you have success, peace, and joy.

Part Four: Testimonials

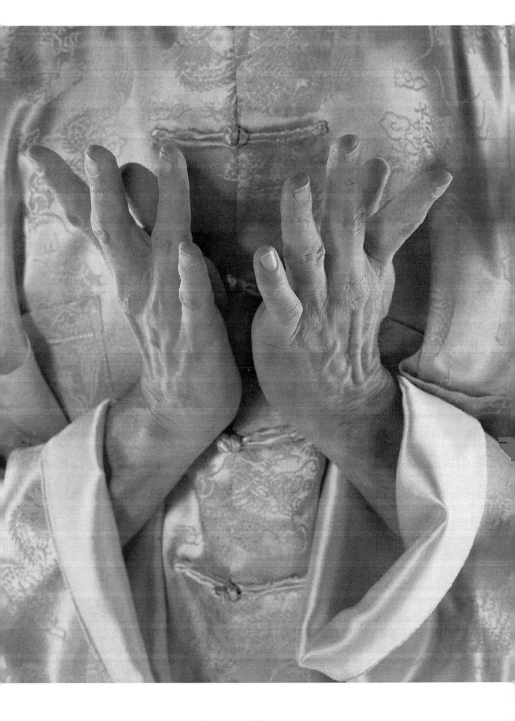

27. People Speak

Professional Recommendations

"One of my polio/post-polio patients has had amazing success with Hsin Tao: she can walk again! ... I am confronted daily with patients that suffer from the after-effects of polio. Is there a publicized document for the public or for physicians? If Hsin Tao can help PPS patients, this must be made public."
Dr. T. Lehmann M.D.

I highly recommend the Hsin Tao exercise technique. In my observation, it produces wide ranging positive results because the 'soul' aspect (i.e. the non-physical attributes of the individual) and physical regeneration are developed simultaneously.
Dr. M. Casey MD

Since I was young, I have had immobile thoracic vertebrae and two years ago I had two hip-joint implants. In my professional experience, blockages of the upper spinal column is common and can remain unnoticed for years, and only after many years, back pain becomes evident either in the lower or upper spine.

The practice of Hsin Tao helps me to retain the natural undulation of the spinal chord (lumbar-dorsal-cervical vertebrae), even at 60 years of age.

This form of physical therapy represents and encourages a general attitude of gentle composure, translated into movements of flowing energy - lightness as a way of meditation.

Ratziel Bander is an excellent teacher. With his precise demonstrations, clear directions and well-directed repetitions, he transmits in only a few hours the capability to practice on your own.

I also recommend this therapy for prevention, before physical limitations are apparent. His new book "The Miracle of Hsin Tao" complements his courses thoroughly for daily use.
Dr. H.G. Füllemann, M.D.

I can say with certainty that the experiences I have had with Hsin Tao go far beyond anything I have had with, for example, Qi Gong and Tai Chi. Hsin Tao is not an exercise program in a conventional sense, rather, it entails letting oneself dive into a physiological process. And it is less physical than it is energetic – as if the movements have a direct connection to the energy system. Sometimes it seems as if every bone is being realigned, straight up into the jawbone and base of the skull. I find it very impressive that it is so easy. At the end of the standing position, when you lay down and simply observe what you feel happening in your body, I could feel the rhythm of brain fluid pulsing, similar to the pulse of the heart. A great sensation that feels as if the tissues are being charged.
Dr. A. von Berghes, M.D., Neurologist/Psychiatrist

Since 1986 I have been learning and teaching Tai Chi Chuan and Qi Gong. The morning after the HSIN TAO Workshop, I started my daily routine with the new exercises, following up with my usual Tai Chi movements. What a surprise! I discovered a spontaneity, ease, and a range unknown to me in my movement, and an effortless control in my pelvic area. True calmness settles in, and there is less fatigue.

I am looking forward to learning some further HSIN TAO exercises and curious what other surprises they have in store for me. Thanks to Ratziel for the clarity and sobriety of his teachings.

Dr. B. Lamy M.D.

As a licensed psychotherapist in California, as well as a postgraduate student in Integrative Body Psychotherapy (a school teaching somatic psychotherapy), I could explain my experience of Hsin Tao in a professional manner. However, I prefer to speak of my experiences with Ratziel from my heart and with much gratitude.

I have been working with Ratziel for several months. I was referred to him by a colleague who was incredibly enthusiastic about the work that Ratziel was doing with her and with others. There was a workshop coming up and I decided to go. I decided to go because I have been chronically ill for a long time.

Years ago I was diagnosed with systemic lupus and fibromyalgia. The most troubling symptoms for me were the debilitating pain and fatigue (among the many other symptoms). The onset of this illness lead me on a journey that lasted years and that included countless doctors and healers trained in Western, Eastern and many other "alternative" modalities. I tried everything available to me over the years to get well. I ultimately found that the only thing that had any positive effect and that did not make my symptoms worse was a variety of prescription medications that do not heal but allow me to function more fully in my life.

Enter Ratziel Bander. I am very excited about the way I am responding to him and to Hsin Tao. In addition to feeling better, I truly am aware of how my total being responds to the techniques. When practicing the breathing and physical movements, I feel deeply rejuvenated and that state of being stays with me beyond the physical practice. Hsin Tao is deeply calming and tranquil and the breathing techniques take me to stillness and a calmer mind quickly. It also helps tremendously in my contemplative practice, my spiritual life and with the activation of chi or life force energy.

I believe that Ratziel and the Hsin Tao techniques are helping me to strengthen as well as rejuvenate my body, mind and spirit. Hsin Tao is perfect for those with physical limitations such as myself because nothing is forced and the movements are gentle and flowing. This enables me to do it at my own pace and capacity. I have been unable to do anything else to strengthen and heal my body without causing what I call a flare... an exacerbation of symptoms. This includes yoga, pilates and even walking.

I am very grateful to be a student of Ratziel's and to be benefiting from the Hsin Tao teachings so profoundly. Ratziel Bander is a wonderful person, a skilled and gifted teacher and he has much to offer to people and to our world.

Sincerely,
  I. Moskowitz, Psychotherapist

Dear Ratziel
I have been practicing Hsin Tao for half of a year. Since then, many symptoms of aging have disappeared: a light incontinence disappeared completely, my balance became noticeably better - I could go up and down a small set of steep stairs with much more confidence - and a pain in my left shoulder that had restricted my mobility for months got better little by little until the pain was completely gone. These results are amazing in and of themselves, but I also noticed that these few easy exercises also resulted in a calmer psyche, I felt stronger and at the same time very relaxed. Even my 83-year-old mother, who suffers pain in her back as a result of severe scoliosis - after one half of a year of Hsin Tao practice, seemed less depressed, more relaxed and open-minded than before. I myself noticed that, for sleeping disorders, the "Saint Prepares Medicine" was a perfect remedy. I am very happy to have discovered Hsin Tao and my morning discipline has reaped rich rewards. I am very thankful for this gift of the old masters.
Dr. B. Thum-Flemming, Psychoanalyst

Dear Ratziel,
I wanted to let you know some of my experience and my thoughts on Hsin Tao.

First, learning and practicing with you has been a wonderful gift. Thank you so much. Second, even though I am not a disciplined person, I find that even with my amount of practice, I move into a state of calm alert very quickly and easily. I have developed a capacity for awareness and presence through my personal work and my studies as a psychotherapist. My Hsin Tao practice deepens both awareness and presence.

I practice and teach INTEGRATIVE BODY PSYCHOTHERAPY and find Hsin Tao a very helpful adjunctive for the clients I have referred to you.

Also, I think this work is appropriate for people experiencing a lack of desire sexually and for those who have a lack of feeling and awareness in the pelvis. I would recommend these people begin in private sessions. If there is a disturbing element associated with the problem then you would be there to facilitate containment and referral, if appropriate.

If the only result of these teachings is to help people find the state of calm alert, that in itself would be wonderful. Now how about the image of millions of human beings living in calm alert? Enough to change the world.

P. Miller, Psychotherapist
Chair, International Association of Integrated Body Psychotherapists

The Hsin Tao techniques taught by Ratziel have a profound essential quality. By that I mean there is a completeness or wholeness in even the simplest of motions, and the integration of a series of movements promotes an energetic awareness that outdistances the imagination. It is helping me embrace the courage needed to receive whatever appears in life, and the wholehearted intention to practice patience (both stunningly worthy qualities in today's world climate). He has my deep gratitude for his service to us all.

Dr. D. Wiess, Psychologist

Ratziel Bander's work and teaching has been a tremendous support and addition to my work as a somatic psychologist and dance/movement therapist. It is fitting with both Western psychological methods and Eastern spiritual practices. I feel honored to have met and studied with him.

M. L. Rand Ph.D., Psychologist

Client Testimonials

I am a former tennis professional who got lupus and fibromyalgia. I tried all different forms of healing exercises. Much to my disappointment when I tried Tai Chi and Chi Gong I got immediately elated then quickly tired and exhausted, and had to go home and sleep for hours. I finally was introduced to Hsin Tao and the results were instant - gentle calmness, balance and a sense of regeneration. Now I am finally able to work on the healing process myself.

F. Troll

I have been practicing Hsin Tao for one and a half years. In mid 2004 I suffered from a paragliding accident - falling 10 meters, which resulted in two fractures on T12 vertebra, one on the 1st vertebra of the tailbone, and one on the breastbone. At that time I made Hsin Tao the focal point of my life.

Within three months, doing two hours of daily Hsin Tao practice, my recovery was complete, and my pain was as good as gone.

I practice gently but regularly and by doing so have been able to regain a healthy back and keep my life as a self-employed heating specialist and musician, fulfilled and in balance.

Thank you Ratziel, and I look forward to the privilege of learning more of this method.
W. Albert

I have been a skier and now snow boarder for over 20 years. Every year for the last twenty years, I have endured severe burning in my legs from lactic acid formation which has limited my ability to enjoy the sport to the fullest. This has occurred in spite of any attempts to get into shape each year. This year is the first time that I did not experience any pain what so ever and did not have to stop. Hsin Tao has given me an unprecedented level of fitness, not only on the mountain but in all of the other sports that I enjoy such as surfing, roller-blading, and volley ball. It has also improved my singing, and I have more energy and peace of mind. Hsin Tao has changed my life!
E. Thiess

"Ratziel, I just I have to tell you about a miracle. After you were here today, with all the work that we did, it was a miracle. When Christiane stood me up tonight, something [in my body] loosened and gave way, and for the first time in my life I was not in such agony when I was up [out of the wheelchair]. Thank you, thank you, thank you."
A. Miller (80-year-old, wheel chair since youth.)

From the first rising out of bed in the morning, to the recreational activities in bed in the late hours of the night, Hsin Tao has enhanced my life experience in remarkable ways—like no other practice that exists, in my opinion. To be specific, within the first few minutes of practice in the early morning, the stiffness and aches of sleep dissolve into a supple spine and limber body.

After following the discipline of Hsin Tao for a few months, in my workouts with my trainer, he continually comments on my increased strength and stamina, that I am showing up the bulky 20-year-old body builders. And more amazing yet, the lubrication I enjoy as a post-menopausal woman will put those manufacturers of slippery products out of business!

R. Rubin

In 2000 at the age of 40 I was struck down with rheumatoid arthritis. It affected practically every joint in my body and I was left unable to do the simplest of tasks and in a great deal of pain. Fortunately I have been blessed in having a wonderful Bowen practitioner who got me back on my feet both literally and emotionally (at my last session he noticed the difference in my energy levels almost immediately and is now very intrigued by Hsin Tao!) and since then have been able to do Pilates classes which have also helped considerably. This is where I was up to when I attended your workshop in June.

The exercises from the start have been a pleasure to perform and apart from feeling a chore or some sort of discipline to be mastered. I feel as if I have been given an enormous piece of the jigsaw, my body seems to be trying very hard to put itself together again. It is a gift. At first I found although I was able to do the moves it was with some discomfort and I was often distracted by the various clicking and crunching from my joints. With daily practice within only a matter of days I began to notice how much more fluid my movements were becoming, my joints felt as if they'd been oiled and it was much quieter on the clicking and crunching front! My hands particularly moved freer and I found to my delight that I could actually place my wrists together as they should be in the routine and not locked at some strange angle. Each day brings more mobility. I am amazed with the amount of extra energy I have and in my general well

being. I feel straighter, stronger and happier. Each small achievement such as managing to break the seal and open a bottle of water unaided makes me more positive and encouraged to keep practicing. I still have some way to go, it is only a month since I started practicing but wow! Today I managed to walk across Hampstead Heath in London, something I always loved and used to do at every opportunity before the arthritis. I stopped regularly and looked around in wonder, my smile stretched from ear-to-ear and I had a tear of joy in my eye - Thank you Ratziel.
    S. Cunningham

Only days after practicing with Ratziel did I begin noticing incredible changes in my body, mind and spirit. Immediately, my lower back ailed by a slipped disk began to stretch and strengthen. Where once I cracked at even the slightest movement, I now flow freely and stand tall. Over the months, breath replaced 16 years of a pack-a-day smoking with no withdrawal symptoms. Having Asthma, this practice decreased my medication intake from two puffs, 4 to 6 times daily, down to 1/2 a puff (one puff is now too much for my body) on rare occasions– THANK GOD. Sleeping was horribly inconsistent before Hsin Tao, and my energy throughout the day was always low. After learning the standing exercises, my energy shot through the roof so drastically that I even had to find ways to expel my suddenly increased sexual vigor. Incredible!
    B. Tortora

Dear Ratziel
I discovered Hsin Tao by accident. A friend called me from Spain and sent me some material about it, saying it was a great thing.

For me, it was the intensity, which I experienced the very day of the Hsin

Tao seminar with Ratziel Bander. It was almost as if it were an energetic initiation. I remember the first day of my practice at home very vividly. The feeling of activation and flow of energy was a sensation I could really feel within ten minutes. To my own surprise, the need to practice daily developed all by itself. I always found the time.

The exercises somehow convey themselves to you. This was sometimes difficult for my mind to accept, as it sometimes had a different concept of "correct". In retrospect, this was especially clear after the first advanced class - it became clear that my body had really understood more than my mind. Somehow, this is a technique that does not recognize an ideal position such as in yoga, for example, but a flow that you "get into".

In addition to the positive effects that are mentioned in the book, I have made the following experiences: all of the tension in my body began to crumble away, buried material came to the forefront. This included physical symptoms (former illnesses, cramping, detoxing) as well as mental (becoming conscious of old, unresolved experiences). There was a noticeable and measurable straightening of the spine.

The change in my physical stance brought about a change in the way I looked at things on a day-to-day basis. Life became easier and friendlier. My personal reactions became more flexible.

I would like especially to note that a very specific change took place in my spirituality. Regular practice resulted in the absolute certainty that godliness is directly within me. Outwardly, this resulted in me separating myself from spiritual teachers and gurus and giving up almost all other practices. Prior to this, meditation had always been a difficult struggle with the thoughts creeping into my mind. Through the movement and the concentration on the movements, meditation came about spontaneously and naturally. It is much easier for me to deal with my hectic business life and to switch over into a sense of tranquility with these movements. Even when I am in the middle of the turbulence, I find that it is easier maintain a calm awareness of the events.

All-in-all, I am very thankful for this gift.
    C. Kuhn

Hello Ratziel,
I was in Munich with my son on June 10th, 2005 in order to learn Hsin Tao with you. This was a particularly special experience and gave me something invaluable. Since then, I have been practicing Hsin Tao every day and today I want to thank you for the strength it gives me.

Recently, I was able to stand up on my legs without support and without pain in my knees - the last time I was able to do that was ten years ago. It was such a wonderful feeling that I am really not able to express it in words.

Heartfelt greetings,
    I. Ischwang

Dear Mr. Bander,
I was fortunate enough to take part in the one-day workshop you gave in Munich, Germany in October and found the experience absolutely overwhelming. I have long wished for some form of "exercise for lazy people" which can be done any place, any time (flexible schedule) and IS EFFECTIVE. To observe your radiance as you demonstrate the three exercises you taught us, and then to feel the deep sense of peace and well being which floods through one's own body and mind, doing them oneself

has opened up a new avenue in my life. It was clear to me that I was in the presence of a master - a very moving experience - and that in Hsin Tao I have found the "next step" on my own path. I am deeply grateful for this encounter. This feels very much like "holy" knowledge. Does that sound exaggerated?

As a lazy person, I have not been practicing as regularly as I intended to, but partly because, once I start, I find it very difficult to stop - it's more than slightly addictive! But even with my occasional forays I have already experienced slight but noticeable physical change. Certain pains disappear, sitting cross-legged is suddenly completely easy, but most striking is the feeling of absolute bliss I experience when doing "The Saint Prepares Medicine". I find myself "grinning all over" and really don't want to stop. So far I have felt no inclination to learn the other exercises out of the book, but prefer to wait until your next visit - in the hope that it will be soon!
    N. Isaacs

I have been practicing Hsin Tao twice daily for 20 to 30 minutes for the past three months. I'm a very active person, I do ballet and have experience with Feldenkrais and am, as a result, very familiar with the way my body moves.

I find the movements in Hsin Tao very easy and virtually anyone can learn them. Even my husband, notoriously unmotivated, has learned them at the seminar and practices together with me.

I have noticed several psychological changes in the course of the last three months that I found and find very important. But the most amazing change for me lately is a very profound physical change.

I have the tendency for a rounded back, though I have always worked on it so that it didn't become too round. This was always difficult and in the last few years it just became worse. According to the doctors and physical therapists, it is impossible for the spine to stretch back into place.

In a relatively short amount of time however, I have noticed a definitive change in my spine. My back is indeed straighter, and I don't have any more problems walking straight up.

Just a while ago, my brother – who hadn't seen me in a while – asked me with a laugh, whether I could still grow at my age, as I appeared somehow taller to him. I found that to be a great bit of feedback. Now, nothing can hinder me with my daily practice.
      H. Zweig

I took 3 private lessons to learn the first three exercises from you. Maybe you remember me - I had acute back problems (herniated discs) at that time. I am very happy and grateful, that I had the opportunity to learn it from you - thank you once again very much! I do the exercises every day and my back is much better now - they are just wonderful and miraculous. Thank you very much, that you bring this spiritual technique and wisdom to us! I hope, that much more people get into contact with the healing power of Hsin Tao!

A lot of light and love
      H. Zürcher

HSIN TAO

Friends - I don't ordinarily promote things via email, but I've had some pretty spectacular results with my experience with this discipline, and feel that it strongly supports anyone looking to enhance their singing experience. Hence, the purpose of this email is to introduce you to the extraordinary work of Ratziel Bander, who teaches a powerful self-healing and regenerative breathing technique called Hsin Tao.

I've experienced the remarkable effects of this discipline as I've practiced it almost daily for the last 3 months. I've experienced an increase in energy, a far more organic relationship with my voice and breath, and renewed vigor while in the act of singing. I strongly recommend it for anyone serious about giving their singing training a strong "jump start". It's simple, enjoyable, and easy to learn.
  W. Hanrahan, *Singing Coach*

Dear Ratziel,
Having returned home after your workshop today i feel moved to write and say thank you so much for sharing this special work with us. I was surprised at the end of the day when someone asked if there was any technique you use to get into meditation, because i found this work took me into meditative states very quickly. I am a meditator already so perhaps that makes the difference. But there were times when i just wanted to abandon all and just stay in the states of bliss that some of the movements lead to. Of course there is still much to learn i realize..........but i was also transported into blissful states of peace just watching you do the demonstrations! Frankly for me exploring consciousness in this way is the whole point, and the healing aspect is a huge added bonus! What a gift! Thank you so much with blessings
  Sue

Dear Ratziel,

It is my pleasure to write this letter of reference and share with you my experience of Hsin Tao. After suffering a major fall and trauma in 1999 I spent approximately 18 months searching for a medical doctor and treatment to alleviate my pain. I couldn't bend forward to tie my shoes, was in constant agony, and as a corporate sales development specialist with clients around the world I had to fly often, and was miserable, uncomfortable and constantly in pain.

Finally, I had an MRI, which determined that I had a compressed disc in my lower back and one in my neck. The consensus amongst the doctors was that since I had nothing broken and was not a candidate for surgery, I was offered pain relievers, a back and neck brace and was told to get used to living with the pain.

Not accepting that diagnosis, I went to chiropractors, acupuncturists and numerous massage therapists searching for "alternative treatments". As part of my journey, I was introduced to yoga, and learned Hatha, Vini, Iyengar, Ashtanga and Restorative Yoga, all which helped to reduce the pain, but none which got me back to normal.

One of my massage therapists recommended that I try a form of exercise called Hsin Tao that was new to America, and fortunately I was still in enough pain that I was open-minded enough to be willing to try it.

Within the first 2-3 private lessons I had with you, I began to feel greater mobility in my back and movement in my neck. Unlike the other forms of yoga that require special clothing and equipment, I found myself practicing a few of the basic Hsin Tao movements in airports, on airplanes, in hotels, even in hallways outside of the rooms I was about to give speeches in. I couldn't believe how simple and fluid the movements are.

To this day, I have not found a better system for self-healing than Hsin Tao, and when you consider that the 2 largest reasons that employees lose work time is due to head aches and back aches, it is my belief that Hsin Tao can be a major help with both of those common ailments, and boost corporate productivity.

More companies are now convinced that there is a link between physically fit bodies and greater productivity therefore they offer exercise classes and basic yoga. It is only logical that people who can tend to their bodies, minds and emotional wellbeing will be even more productive, therefore I highly urge any intelligent, open-minded executive to implement a Hsin Tao program and monitor the results.

I love working with my clients and giving them the gift of wealth, but to think that you give people the gift of health, what employer wouldn't want to have the opportunity to increase their employees health and boost morale at the same time?

I would be happy to further discuss my findings with anyone in need of additional information.

Respectfully,
    L. Atlas

Hsin Tao surprises me every time I do it. Tonight I wanted to quickly warm up before doing the movements. I sat down on my pillow and began the breathing exercise. In about a minute I was completely relaxed and my mind was absolutely quiet. My days are usually pretty hectic, so for me to be able to reach a peaceful state of mind in such a short time is a huge development.

J. Foshey

The exercises not only calm my mind and take me into a meditative state, but they increase my overall energy. I find that I actually need less sleep. With each day's practice I feel an increase in energy flowing into my body through the 4th eye. It is as if my 4th eye is opening like a flower to the sun, and the warmth on my forehead is palpable after each Hsin Tao practice/meditation. I can also feel an increase in the warmth of my energy center. And when doing the arm movements I can actually feel my arms and hands tingle. More and more there is the physical sensation that I am moving energy with my hands. My Hsin Tao practice and meditation sessions have become the highlight of my day. I truly look forward to them.

I work in an uncertain and stressful profession where inflated egos tend to run rampant, and insecurity rides like a pestering monkey on one's back. Over the past few years I have been making a real effort to relinquish my expectations and allow things to ebb and flow naturally. I feel that the practice of Hsin Tao has been wonderfully helpful in my effort toward non-attachment and the release of my ego.

I am excited about continuing to learn more of Hsin Tao and to go deeper with my practice.

J. G. Davis

I am totally ecstatic about Mr. Bander's book. I have been practicing Hsin Tao for two weeks, meaning actually only two exercises once or twice a day and they do me a lot of good. I have neurodermitis, asthma, depressions and panic attacks. I don't think the book can substitute for a seminar, yet one can still get good results. After an itch attack, I am often not able to properly move my hands or arms. I haven't been able to work miracles yet, but afterward I usually feel as if my skin has acquired a protective coating and I can move around for quite a while without it pulling or aching.

Many kind greetings,
        A. Moll

I came to see Ratziel to learn about Hsin Tao in December of 2001. As a pragmatist and somewhat materialistic, I was completely dismissive of anything to do with eastern healing. After the first 75-minute lesson, I felt an emotional and physiological shift in my soul. I have continued lessons with Ratziel since then and can honestly say that the practice of Hsin Tao has been one of the single most influential and life changing efforts that I have ever made. Hsin Tao has allowed me to become more unified, whole, and stronger. I have a sense of inner courage, that I have never had before and have dedicated much time in the promotion of the practice in southern California. I strongly recommend the practice to anyone and feel that if a skeptic like me can benefit, anyone can.
        C. Fernandes

It is almost two weeks since I attended your workshop in Woodland Hills and I feel great. I believe I told you that I was diagnosed with either a herniated disk or a spur in my neck several years ago. I had an MRI and was told by the doctor that I should have either an operation or steroid shots to rid myself of the pain. I declined both suggestions and he gave me several different types of anti inflammatories to try. Each caused all kinds of side effects and I quit taking them. The doctor told me, that no matter what I did, I would always have pain holding my head erect and tingling in my arm. I discovered MSM with chicken collagen, which alleviated the pain, but has required daily usage. While they are not expensive, the pills do cost $20 to $30 per month. I have tried not using them in the past, but after four or five days I begin to experience discomfort in my neck, back and left arm.

I felt so good after learning Zen Buddhist Yoga that I thought I would just see what would happen if I practiced the techniques and quit using the MSM/chicken collagen. The results have been great. I am beginning to stand straighter and I have not experienced any pain or discomfort in my back, neck or arm. In addition, all the little aches and pains that come with being 70 years old are quickly going away. Another plus is the increase in energy. Each day I am gaining more energy and the feeling of well-being that goes with it.

Thank you so much for sharing your knowledge with me. I have added Hsin Tao to my daily schedule of meditation. I am currently using the techniques for about 30 minutes, twice a day.

With deep love and gratitude,
    C. Campbell

For many years I have suffered of heavy migraines that sent me sometimes to bed, even. After having excluded all dairy products from my foods, there was an improvement for some time. However, during these last six months I was hit as often as every other day by megrims. Shortly after the HSIN TAO workshop, I noticed that I was able to stop the megrim immediately at its beginning by doing the exercises. Suddenly, I could identify the source and thus avoid some attacks all together. I am so happy to be able at last to control my megrims myself! On top of it I feel lighter, I am less worried and am more trusting in life and me. Heartfelt thanks for having brought Ratziel to Switzerland!

A week ago, my 19-year-old son was torn away from this life by a train engine. Even in this tragic situation the HSIN TAO exercises help me to go on living and to stay in touch with my son.

I. Badeaux

In March 1998 I started to suffer from strong back pains. Since the pains persisted, I had several sessions of acupuncture and mesotheraphie where they injected several products into my muscles and joints. The next day after the treatment, I felt better, but the pain always returned, especially in bed. I have always been sportive, swimming regularly, walking, roller-skating and skiing so the back pain didn't come from these sports. I stopped all the treatments after 4 years because nothing worked. I even changed my bed, mattress, and pillows and slept with a belt around my abdomen to keep my lower back warm. Nothing worked. I changed my chair in my office, and continued to wear flat shoes with no heels, no carrying of heavy bags. I changed to carrying a backpack instead of a purse.

My natural doctor examined my teeth and sent me to a dentist who was also a natural doctor. The x-rays discovered a infected root, which the dentist treated, and he changed a metal filling to resin. After all was settled, my back pains were less but always strongly present when I woke up each morning. My natural doctor insisted I see another osteopath. I did. Nothing changed.

On November 9, 2002 I went to a one-day workshop to learn HSIN TAO. The back pain continued. I changed the cushion I was using to practice the simple breathing and movements. Three days after the workshop I woke up with no back pain. Curious to see if it was the practice of HSIN TAO I lessened the time I practiced. The back pain returned immediately. Now I practice about 20 to 30 minutes every morning. Sometimes I practice a short moment before going to bed. I wake up each morning without any back pain and nor do I have any back pain during the whole day. Thank you Ratziel!
    S. Bridel

As designer I am, like many other artists, not very securely anchored in this world. This results in some tricky situations in my family with our little ones, as well as in business meetings. Now, with the Hsin Tao exercises, I feel much more present and in harmony with my body and I am again able to breathe freely, after several years where my nose was heavily blocked up. Last week my father passed away and I am still astonished how I lived through this emotional time from the deathbed to the funeral with such equanimity. The unceasing questions of my kids and their crying are also easier for me to bear. Now, I stay "cool" longer. I just cannot fathom all the changes these simple, elegant exercises may still bring about in me.
    J. Eichmann

For more testimonials see www.hsintao.com

End Notes

1. Yoga posture

2. Power Yoga is a modern development of Ashtanga Yoga. It is based on Hatha yoga postures, but is extremely rigorous and strenuous.

3. The original Shaolin Monastery is in the mountainous region of Henan province. Hsin literally means "men in the mountains".

4. In recent years, the Chinese government has reopened and operates the original Shaolin monastery in Henan province. The Communist government strictly controls it through a series of proxies. Many remarkable feats of martial arts are being achieved there. Some of which are being exported as travelling shows. Nowadays, the philosophical nature of the work within the monastery walls is leaning more freely toward Buddhist and Taoist thought, although communist party guidelines regarding religion and spirituality are still government policy. Hsin Tao is rumoured to be in the monastery once again. It is incorporated into other martial techniques for the more dedicated practitioners. Primarily it is used for emotional healing, although the spectrum of the technique's regenerative properties may still be whispered and encouraged to a select few. The torture, disappearance, and 're-education' in recent years of thousands of China's Falong Gong practitioners, as reported in Australia's news media, indicates that China is still a dangerous place for those who think outside the limitations of proletariat ideals. As such, the truth about Hsin Tao on its home territory remains a mystery to this day.

5. A specific type of directional and healing vital energy, that flows along specific bodily pathways (meridians) and through the bones.

NOTES

NOTES

NOTES

NOTES

2699944

Made in the USA